A storyteller's guide to the gospels

How to bring
65 Gospel stories
to life

Owen Shelley

Scripture Union

Scripture Union books are published in Australia by
Scripture Union Australia
Resources for Ministry Unit
PO Box 77
Lidcombe
NSW 1825, Australia

Scripture taken from the HOLY BIBLE, NEW INTERNATIONAL
VERSION copyright © 1973, 1978, 1984 International Bible Society,
unless otherwise stated. Used by permission of Zondervan Bible
Publishers.

National Library of Australia Cataloguing-in-Publication Data

Shelley, Owen
A storyteller's guide to the gospels

ISBN 0 949720 85 2

Bible. N.T. Gospels – Children's sermons. 2. Bible. N.T. Gospels –
Study and teaching. 3. Emotions – Religious aspects – Christianity
– Study and teaching. 4. Spiritual healing - Bible teaching.
I. Scripture Union Australia. II. Title.

131

Cover Design by Ivan Smith, Communique Graphics
Typesetting by Melbourne Media Services

Contents

Dedicated to the memory of my sister, Lyn – an encourager

Other books by the author:
Chalk and Talk, Scripture Union, 1996

My thanks to Joan Llewellyn and Peggy Smith for typing,
and Rena Pritchard for editorial help.

Introduction to Imaginative Presentation

'I believe in heaven and all that. It's the stories about Jesus that I've got my doubts about!'

When a fifteen years old girl made this remark in a discussion group it brought immediate assent from others in the group. The girls were students at an Anglican school where religious instruction was given regularly and yet they were expressing doubt about the central fact of the Christian faith, the existence of Jesus as an historical person. Those involved in religious instruction will know that this is not an isolated incident.

Similar expressions of doubt are common among children in their teenage years. The reason for this is complex, but one contributing factor is our failure to present the story in a way that grips the imagination of students. Much of our teaching is given in formal lectures, resulting in boredom and scepticism. The solution is not always obvious.

Speaking at a training conference for scripture teachers, I said that we needed to present lessons in an imaginative and interesting way. 'That's all right for people like you', announced one delegate. 'You all tell us that we have to present imaginative lessons but I'm not an imaginative person. I sit down to prepare my lesson and say to myself "I've got to be imaginative", but truthfully, I don't know where to start.'

I went home thinking about the problem. Is imagination the province of a limited few or is it something we all can learn? I believe it can be learned if we keep in mind these four keys to imaginative presentation:

- Facts,
- Flow,
- Focus, and
- Feelings.

I wish to enlarge on each of these.

Marshalling the facts

Often events in the gospels are only stated briefly so that when you come to teach you find that only limited information is provided about various incidents. To gather the maximum amount of material you need to:

Examine all the available reports

Note these parallel references. For example, there are three accounts of Jesus calming the storm – Matthew 8:23-27, Luke 8:22-25 and Mark 4:35-41. Notice the following details:

- The event took place 'when evening came' (Mark) **Time**
- The trip was at Jesus' suggestion – 'let us go over to the other side' (Matthew, Mark, Luke) **Minor detail**
- Prior to setting out, Jesus had been preaching to a crowd (Luke) – 'leaving the crowd behind' (Mark) **Time – Minor detail**
- Probably Jesus had been speaking from the boat – 'they took him along, just as he was, in the boat' (Mark) **Minor detail**
- A number of people accompanied him – 'there were also other boats with him' (Mark) **Minor detail**
- The boat was driven by sail –'As they sailed' (Luke)
- The storm was unexpected – 'without warning a furious storm came up' (Matthew, Mark) **Key fact**
- The storm was so intense the boat was in danger of being swamped – 'the waves broke over the boat' (Matthew, Mark, Luke)
- Despite the intensity of the storm, the Lord was sound asleep (Matthew, Luke) in the stern of the boat (Mark) – 'sleeping on a cushion' (Mark) **Fact and minor detail**
- The terrified disciples woke Jesus up. The three accounts vary at this point (Matthew – 'Lord, save us! We're going to drown'), (Mark – 'Teacher, don't you care if we drown?'), (Luke – 'Master, we're going to drown') **Parallel accounts**

- Jesus 'rebuked the wind and the waves' (Matthew, Luke), 'Quiet, be still' (Mark) **Significant detail**
- He rebuked the disciples for their lack of faith – 'Why are you so afraid? Do you still have no faith?' (Matthew, Mark, Luke) **Significant detail**
- The disciples were both astonished and terrified, expressing their amazement with – 'What kind of man is this? Even the winds and waves obey him.' (Matthew, Mark, Luke) **Significant detail**

Glancing back through this list, what did you find significant? Perhaps you overlooked the presence of a small flotilla of boats, that Jesus was asleep on a cushion or the fact that his supernatural display of power filled the disciples with fear. Some of these details may seem insignificant but they help us to capture the reality of the occasion.

For example, think about the variations of the disciples' terror as they woke Jesus. Recognise that as storytellers, this information can be used to give the impression of people all gabbling at Jesus at once. Obviously they would not all have used the same words – this would be most unnatural – so don't give the audience the false impression that they were speaking in unison.

If you examine all of the accounts, you will gain greater insight into the spiritual lesson the story is stressing. For example, I have often asked scripture teachers to identify the teaching Jesus gave on the occasion of feeding five thousand people. Their replies vary from 'God can provide our needs' to 'Jesus can take and use whatever we offer him'. These are aspects of teaching that can be seen in this story, but Jesus used the incident in an entirely different way.

To discover the stress, turn to John's account (John 6: 1-15). Note that the other gospels report what happened without comment, while John reports the reaction of the people who witnessed the miracle: 'Surely this is the Prophet who is to come into the world' (v. 14). When Jesus realised that the people intended to make him king 'by force' (v. 15), he headed for the hills but even there he did not manage to elude them. They tracked him down at Capernaum and asked: 'Rabbi, when did you get here?' (v. 25)

Jesus' reply contains a rebuke: 'You are looking for me, not because you saw the miraculous signs but because you ate the loaves and had your fill' (v. 26). He seems to infer that they were hoping for another free feed. His words, 'Do not work for food that spoils, but for food that endures to eternal life' (v. 27), is still valid teaching in today's society. So much emphasis is placed on material possessions being the key to happiness, as can be seen in the TV advertisement, 'Go Lotto, go Lotto, you're mad if you don't.'

Jesus then used the occasion to point out that only he can satisfy our spiritual hunger: 'I am the bread of life. He who comes to me will never go hungry, and he who believes in me will never be thirsty' (v. 35).

Trace other references in the record to the incident you are describing

John is the only writer who reports the raising of Lazarus (see John 11:1-45) which continues into the following chapter. There he describes a return visit by Jesus to the family in Bethany and reports that Lazarus was one of the group 'reclining at the table with him' (John 12:2). Lazarus received much attention as what we would call, 'Exhibit A' – a large crowd of curiosity seekers gathered not only to see Jesus but 'also to see Lazarus whom he had raised from the dead' (John 12:9). Poor Lazarus – having just survived one death the chief priests were planning to kill him again, because of the effect his returning from the dead was having on the people (vv. 10-11). Was he was aware of this?

The story is still not complete as there is another reference to the incident later in Chapter 12 (vv. 17-18). When crowds waving palm branches greeted Jesus, those who had witnessed the raising of Lazarus were among the most vocal.

Note the minor details

Throughout the biblical record the writers pop in seemingly insignificant facts which give their reports the ring of authenticity. If these accounts were fictitious one would not expect to find references of this sort. Consider the following examples:

- During the storm on the lake, Jesus is reported as sleeping 'on a cushion' in the stern of the boat (Mark 4:38). It only takes a moment's reflection to realise that the transom would be very uncomfortable without a cushion.
- When the crowd of 5,000 men and their families were to be fed, they were directed to sit in groups to facilitate the distribution of the bread and fish. This would be reasonably comfortable as the grass was 'green' at that location (Mark 6:39).
- When Jesus spoke with the Samaritan woman, their conversation was interrupted by the return of Jesus' friends. John records that the woman hurried back to the city 'leaving her water jar' behind (John 4:28) to report her discovery. Again this action is obvious – she was in a hurry. Carrying her water jar would have hindered her, slowing her down.

Reflecting on such details can give us deeper insight into these incidents.

Check the time

'What's the time?' is a question constantly repeated in everyday life so the frequent reference to the time when various events took place is another pointer to their authenticity. Some reflection on the references to time gives further insight into the happenings.

- The flotilla of boats set out to cross the lake 'when evening came' (Mark 4:35). By the time the squall blew up, it may have been dark. Having had the experience of being caught at night in a canoe in the middle of a lake in when a 'southerly buster' blew up, I can identify with the disciples' terror when the squall hit, and how darkness would add to it.

- It was 'evening' (Matthew 14:15) when the 5,000 were fed, a time when the people would begin to feel hungry.
- Matthew 21:18-22 reports the strange event of the unproductive fig tree. 'Early in the morning, as [Jesus] was on his way back to the city, he was hungry' (v. 18). It would appear that he had missed his breakfast that day and on finding no fruit on the tree, caused the tree to wither before their eyes.
- John reports that the meeting with the Samaritan woman took place 'about the sixth hour' – midday (John 4:6). It would seem reasonable to suggest that she came to the well at that hot, unpleasant hour to avoid meeting her neighbours.
- In the recorded events surrounding the trial and crucifixion of Jesus there are frequent references to the time. We know from John's report that he was arrested at night by 'a detachment of soldiers ... carrying torches, lanterns and weapons' (John 18:3).
- The trials before both Annas and Caiaphas took place during the night while Peter sat huddled around a fire in the courtyard. 'A servant girl saw him seated there in the firelight' (Luke 22:56) and identified him. And when Peter heard the rooster crow (Luke 22:60), it would have been in the very early hours of the morning.
- It was still 'very early in the morning' (Mark 15:1,2) that the chief priests and the members of the Sanhedrin (Council) made the decision to hand Jesus over to Pontius Pilate for judgment. Was Pilate normally an early riser **or did he stay up late at night**? Had the elders arranged with him the previous day to meet them at this early hour?
- Later in the account we find references to 'the third hour', 'the sixth hour' and 'the ninth hour' (Mark 15:25,33,34), giving us some understanding of the length of time that our Lord endured the agony of the cross. Jesus was crucified at the third hour, i.e. nine o'clock in the morning.

Taking into account all that happened in the preceding hours of darkness – the trial before Pilate and a detour for cross examination by Herod with 'many questions' (Luke 23:9), we realise why the report says that it was 'at daybreak' (Luke 22:66) that the trial began.

- The resurrection record also makes frequent reference to the time of events. The women who went to anoint Jesus' body arrived at his tomb 'just after sunrise' (Mark 16:2).
- By contrast, Cleopas and his companion met the Lord much later in the day. 'Stay with us,' they urged him, 'for it is nearly evening; the day is almost over' (Luke 24:29).
- Then, 'On the evening of that first day of the week' (John 20:19) Jesus appeared to his disciples in the upper room.

Identify the significant

John has helpfully provided us with a summary of the intention of the gospel writers. He says, 'Jesus did many other miraculous signs in the presence of his disciples which are not recorded in this book. But these are written that you may believe that Jesus is the Christ, the Son of God, and that by believing you may have life in his name' (John 20:30-31).

Our purpose is similar. Through recounting the stories graphically we seek to open the eyes of those we teach to Jesus as the Son of God. Let us now observe Paul in his prison cell in Rome as he gathers around him the leaders of the Jews.

'From morning till evening he explained and declared to them the kingdom of God and tried to convince them about Jesus from the Law of Moses and from the Prophets' (Acts 28:23).

For the next two years he 'preached the kingdom of God and taught about the Lord Jesus Christ' (Acts 28:31). It is plain from this report that Paul knew what he was on about.

Some years ago I set a group of Bible College students an assignment. They were to prepare an outline of a series of talks to be given at a children's weekend house party. To my surprise, when I came to mark their work I found some had done a whole series on creation and other topics, but never once in the whole of the material had they mentioned the name of Jesus.

The following year with the next batch of students at that college, I included a lecture on the 'Centrality of Jesus' to encourage them to see that our teaching, especially in missions, holiday activities, schools work and so on, needed to focus on Jesus. This group was given a similar assignment and to my dismay there were still some who made no mention of the Lord Jesus in their outlines.

As you study the record of Jesus' actions watch for the phrase or sentence that emphasises the significance of who Jesus is, keeping in mind Paul's question, 'How, then, can they believe in the one of whom they have not heard?' (Romans 10:14)

Consider these examples:
'We have never seen anything like this' (Mark 2:12).

'What kind of man is this? Even the wind and the waves obey him' (Matthew 8:27).

'Surely this is the Prophet who is to come into this world' (John 6:14).

'Lord to whom shall we go? You have the words of eternal life. We believe and know that you are the Holy One of God' (John 6:68,69).

'No one ever spoke the way this man does' (John 7:46).

'Then the man said, "Lord I believe" and he worshipped him' (John 9:38).

Planning the flow

Every lesson needs a framework on which to hang a pattern or progression of events. Each needs:
- An Introduction
- Action
- A Climax
- A Conclusion

If the teacher can find some feature of the story that creates a link throughout, this helps to give the presentation a natural flow.

As an example let us look at the incident of the healing of blind Bartimaeus. In his account, Mark reports that Bartimaeus 'jumped to his feet' to meet Jesus, 'throwing his cloak aside' (Mark 10:50). This action of throwing his cloak aside can provide the link to build the progression of our story.

To motivate their interest, question the children about rubbish left in the street, such as an old car dumped in a back lane. Go on to say that if you had entered the gateway of the city of Jericho many years ago, you just might have noticed an old coat lying by the roadside, a coat that used to belong to an old blind beggar called Bartimaeus (Luke 18:35-43). Then describe Bartimaeus' plight and the hope that rose up in his heart when he heard that Jesus of Nazareth was passing by.

Action
Describe the way Bartimaeus kept on shouting to Jesus for help while the crowd kept trying to shut him up. His persistence was rewarded when the crowd said to him, 'Cheer up! Get on your feet! He's calling you!' So, throwing his cloak aside, he hurried forward to meet Jesus.

Climax
If there is one action that demonstrates that Bartimaeus believed that Jesus could restore his sight, it is this record that notes he threw his cloak aside. A blind person putting their cloak down, would never find it again. Then, following a brief conversation with Jesus, Bartimaeus had his eyesight restored and 'followed Jesus along the road'.

Conclusion

I wonder if Bartimaeus went back for his cloak. Possibly not – it was most likely left lying in the gateway. People passing later that day might have noticed it and said, 'Look at that grubby old coat. It belonged to Bartimaeus. What an amazing thing that Jesus did for him. Jesus really must be the Son of God.'

Note from this outline that the references to the cloak provide the link between introduction, climax and conclusion, creating a good flow to the account.

Choosing the focus

There is a paradox in today's society – while many children are completely ignorant of the gospel story, others are so familiar with it that for them it has become boring and irrelevant.

Imagine the following scenario:
At Christmas time, Jenny attends Sunday school and is given a lesson based on the Christmas story. The following Tuesday evening she attends the local Girls' Brigade where the story of Christmas becomes the focus of the devotional time. On Wednesday Jenny is chosen for the part of Mary in a nativity play at her school, and on Friday her scripture teacher's lesson is on the events of Christmas.

Imagine the difficulty faced by the scripture teacher, who has to capture her interest about something she has already heard three times that week, not to mention last Christmas and the one before that.

Our task as teachers is to find some way to focus attention on the story using new angles to stimulate interest. One method is to focus upon an aspect that might be overlooked by other teachers. For example, the incident of the triumphal entry into Jerusalem is well known. A friend asked for my help to find a new focus for her class of junior teens. We came up with the idea of focusing on the question, 'Who was there?' We assumed that the children knew all the details of the people waving branches and shouting out their welcome as Jesus passed by on the donkey, so we condensed these aspects of the story into one brief sentence, then asked them, 'Who was there?'

We discovered four categories of people in the crowd – the **ignorant**, the **informed**, the **irritated** and the **interested**.

The **ignorant** asked, 'Who's this?' (Matthew 21:10); the **informed** knew all about Jesus as they had been present at the raising of Lazarus (John 12:17); the **irritated** Pharisees asked him to rebuke the disciples for their enthusiasm (Luke 19:39) and the **interested** Greeks requested to be introduced to Jesus (John 12:20,21).

Using this angle on the story my friend maintained the interest of the class throughout the whole lesson, even though these junior teenagers had heard the story every year since the time they were small. When I used this example at a teacher training session, a church minister said, 'That's a terrific outline. I'll use that for my sermon next Palm Sunday. But what do you tell them next year?' This is the crux of the problem. I answered it by saying, 'For a class of junior teens you could construct an interesting lesson around Jesus' prophecy relating to the overthrow of Jerusalem in Luke 19:41-44. By gleaning some facts from the historical records about the destruction of Jerusalem by the Romans, you could bring an entirely different focus to the story. But please don't ask me what to teach the year after that. That would take a considerable amount of thought!'

Reporting the feelings

From the record, we know nothing about the appearance of each of the people in the gospel story, but we do have strong indications concerning their character. Like us, they experienced all our common emotions – excitement, surprise, joy, amazement, disappointment, fear, terror, anger and concern. In studying the record, look out for references to emotion and, as you tell the story, try to depict them through the tone of your voice, your facial expressions and gesture.

Here are some of the ways you can gain insight into the feelings of participants in the gospel drama:

Through their reported actions
For example, study the following actions:
- 'A man with leprosy came to him and **begged** him **on his knees**' (Mark 1:40).
- 'Then the woman ... came **trembling** and **fell** at his feet' (Luke 8:47).
- 'He [Zacchaeus] came down at once and **welcomed him gladly**' (Luke 19:6).
- 'They stood still, **their faces downcast**' (Luke 24:17).

Through their reported emotions
- When Jesus healed the man with the withered hand, his enemies 'were **furious** and began to discuss with one another what they might do to Jesus' (Luke 6:11).
- At Simon the Pharisee's house, as the woman 'stood behind him at his feet **weeping**, she began to **wet his feet** with her tears' (Luke 7:38).
- 'They were **delighted** and agreed to give him money' (Luke 22:5).
- When the women reported that the tomb was empty the disciples 'did not believe the women, because their words **seemed** to them **like nonsense**' (Luke 24:11).

Through a study of their conversation
Studying the conversation enables the storyteller to interpret the mood of the occasion. What tone would the participants have used in the following?

'Nazareth! Can anything good come from there?' (John 1:46)

'It has taken forty-six years to build this temple, and you are going to raise it in three days?' (John 2:20)

'If you had been here, my brother would not have died' (John 11:21).

'No, you shall never wash my feet' (John 13:8).

'Am I a Jew?' (John 18:35)

'They have taken my Lord away, and I don't know where they have put him' (John 20:13).

To me, these examples indicate scepticism, ridicule, irritation, indignation, disdain and distress.

Through the reports of the emotional reactions of Jesus

It is obvious that Jesus felt deeply about those in need. Mark reports that when he sensed that the occupants of the synagogue were more concerned with the legal aspects of the Sabbath than the plight of the man with the crippled hand, 'he looked round at them in **anger**' and became '**deeply distressed** at their stubborn hearts' (Mark 3:5).

After Lazareth had died, John reports that when Jesus saw the distress of Mary, he 'wept' (John 11:35).

Turning to the account of his suffering in the garden of Gethsemane, we catch a glimpse of the anguish Jesus experienced at that time. Mark reports him as saying: 'My soul is overwhelmed with sorrow to the point of death' (Mark 14:34).

Luke gives us further insight in this, recording that 'being in anguish, he prayed more earnestly, and his sweat was like drops of blood falling to the ground' (Luke 22:44). When describing this sacred moment, remember to report it with a due sense of awe and reverence.

As the storyteller develops the habit of watching for references to emotion and seeks to depict these, characters will be brought to life and the interest of the audience captured. To counter the over-familiarity with the gospel stories of some children who as described earlier tend to feel 'they know it all', I point out that they don't 'know it all'! Scripture teachers need to dig more deeply into the gospel mine and bring facts to their attention that they have not known before.

In the comments that follow, we will look at some of the major events in the life of Jesus under two main headings, 'Charting the action' and 'Noting the emotion'. In some instances there are 'Extra comments' and a section entitled 'For children'. The latter suggests a different focus for when these stories are communicated to children for we need to be clear about our purpose in recounting these events. Some of the lengthier accounts provide an adequate base for a lesson or sermon while briefer incidents may need to be linked together to illustrate an appropriate application.

The stories

THE BIRTH OF JOHN THE BAPTIST

 Focus Passage: Luke 1:5-25, 1:57-66

This is the curtain raiser event of the New Testament, the preliminary game preceding the main event. As such it is often ignored. But what it reveals is significant, and this will have a bearing on the report of the birth of Jesus that is to follow. In that unfolding drama John will have a role, for it is he who will urge people to prepare for what will be revealed as the most important event in history.

Immediately after Zechariah is informed of John's approaching birth, scenes of high drama begin. Imagine the scene – a crowd of devout worshippers is gathering round the entrance to the Temple, awaiting the emergence of the priest from the Holy place, where he had been rostered on to burn incense.

'What's happening?' ask the people. 'Why is Zechariah taking so long?' 'He's been inside the Temple for ages!'

'He's one of the older priests – they all seem to stretch it out a bit when they are on duty.' 'Look! Here he comes now!'

Zechariah comes stumbling down the Temple steps. The waiting crowd gasps with astonishment.

'Zechariah! What's the matter? What's happened?' people ask as the old man signals wildly with his hands. 'He's pointing at his mouth! Can't he talk? Get him to a doctor,' say his friends, gathering around to help him.

Charting the action

Luke introduces us to the elderly priest, Zechariah, chosen 'by lot ... to go into the temple to burn incense' (v. 9). While performing this duty, regarded as a once in a lifetime honour by those selected, 'an angel of the Lord appeared to him' (v. 11).

The angel had made a special visit to inform him that his wife Elizabeth would conceive and bear a son. Now, Zechariah and his wife were well aware of their ages. Elizabeth was too old to bear children, so naturally Zechariah was sceptical. 'How can I be sure of this?' he asked (v. 18). Gabriel was obviously unimpressed by Zechariah's response, so punished him for his doubts, informing him that he would be unable to speak until the baby was born.

 Noting the emotion

Artists tend to think in pictures. When describing something to an artist friend, his busy pen produces an illustration of it within minutes. Few have this ability, but those of us who aspire to be storytellers need to be able to visualise in our minds the scene we wish to retell. Our task is to paint word pictures of the events, and if we take careful note of references to emotion in the record, this will help us to do this.

John's birth is not often used by storytellers, but this incident is an excellent starting point for learning the exercise as it bristles with references to emotion – fear, scepticism, surprise, astonishment, awe and joy are all there.

As you study these notes, keep your Bible open at the passage. If you wish, underline any emotional clues you find described in the text as this can help implant the word pictures in your memory.

Luke records that when Zechariah saw the angel 'he was startled and gripped with fear' (1:12). In his greeting, the angel seeks to reassure Zechariah. 'Do not be afraid. Your prayer has been heard' (v. 13). When he is told that he will have a son, Zechariah's **scepticism** must have been obvious, either from the tone of his voice, or in the expression of his face. Contrast this with Mary's response in a similar situation – Mary receives neither rebuke nor penalty from the angel.

Zechariah's encounter with Gabriel must have extended the usual time it took for the priest to perform the duty of incense lighting, for the crowd outside began 'wondering why he stayed so long in the temple' (v. 21). When he staggered out and they discovered he had become dumb, they 'realised' he had seen a vision' (v. 22).

The record reveals the **shame** that resulted in those days from having no children. So when Elizabeth conceived, it was cause for much **rejoicing**: 'The Lord has … taken away my **disgrace** among the people' (v. 25).

Towards the end of the chapter the birth of John is reported (vv. 57-66). On the eighth day following, neighbours and relatives arrived for the traditional circumcision and naming ceremony. They automatically assumed that baby would be named after his father. At this suggestion, Elizabeth **disagrees** most **emphatically**. 'No!' she announces bluntly, 'his name is John' (v. 60 CEV). This break with tradition does not appear to have any logic to the relatives who argue that 'no-one in your family has ever been named John' (v. 61 CEV). A sign language conversation with Zechariah follows and he signals for a writing tablet. Then to 'everyone's **astonishment**' Zechariah writes, 'His name is John!' (v. 63).

Instantly, Zechariah's speech is restored and he bursts into praise to God. The neighbours were all 'filled with awe' and the incident became the talk of the district for 'people were **talking** about all these things' (v. 65). The birth of John caused quite a stir for 'everyone who heard this **wondered** about it' (v. 66).

 ### For children

While this incident is sometimes included in series of children's stories, it should not be taught as an isolated event.

Children can confuse it with the story of the birth of Jesus, which will give them a muddled understanding of that event.

 Extra comment

The angel's speech, verses 13-17, repays study. It clearly details the purpose Jesus has for John, which is 'to make ready a people prepared for the Lord'. The message Zechariah wrote on the tablet reads 'John, his name is', which when translated literally from Greek into English, emphasises his name. Remember that John's parents' did not choose his name – Zechariah was given this name by the angel Gabriel, in dramatic circumstances.

THE BIRTH OF JESUS

 Focus Passage: *Matthew 1:18—2:23*
                                        Luke 1:26-45, 2:1-20

Sometimes as the festive season approaches, I receive a phone call from a friend in ministry asking me for ideas for his Christmas sermon. All who are in ministry regularly face the problem that events surrounding the birth of Jesus are well known, even to many non-churchgoers. This may explain why the reports of the nativity have been embellished more than any other parts of the Biblical record.

I recall attending an infants' school assembly where the speaker spoke at length about the 'dear little donkey' that Mary rode. Yet when you read the actual reports you find they are stark, and donkeys and camels don't get a mention.

 Noting the emotion

Luke commences this section with the words 'in the sixth month', referring to Elizabeth's pregnancy. Again the angel Gabriel is the divine messenger, informing Mary that she has been especially chosen to be the mother of the one who will be 'the Son of the Most High'. Mary accepts this with the words 'I am the Lord's servant. May it be to me as you have said' (1:32,38). Following this encounter with the angel, Mary hurries off to Elizabeth's home to share the news, staying three months with her before returning home.

To place the events in sequence, turn to Matthew, who provides insight into Joseph's reaction to Mary's pregnancy (1:18-24). It is obvious that he does not consider himself to be the father of the child, yet he is respectful of Mary and does not wish to add to her troubles by making her condition public at this time.

Luke does not mention this. He takes up the story again by reporting the Roman census, the birth and place of the birth of the baby, the appearance of the angel to the shepherds announcing the birth and their subsequent journey to Bethlehem to find the baby (2:5-20). The narrative at this point is brief: 'They hurried off and found Mary and Joseph, and the baby, who was lying in the manger' (v.16). This brevity makes the search sound simple but it must have been complicated. Imagine them trying to find them in the dark in a town full of visitors, enquiring at various places before finding the right one:

'Hey landlord! Has there been a baby born here tonight?'

'A baby! How would I know? Why do you ask?'

'We are looking for a woman who may have given birth to a baby tonight.'

'A couple were here earlier, the woman looked as though she was close to giving birth but we didn't have room for them. Try the courtyard; they could be camped there.'

After looking for and finding the baby, the shepherds returned to their sheep, on the way spreading the word about all that they had seen and heard.

It is Matthew who reports the visit of the Wise Men (Matthew 2:1-12). 'We three Kings of Orient are' is the less than accurate opening line of a well-known Christmas carol. It reinforces some of the myths surrounding these mysterious visitors from the East. One early tradition suggests that there may have been ten wise men, not three. That the rank of king is bestowed upon them stems mainly from the value of the gifts the men brought with them. In art they are depicted astride elaborately decorated camels, often portrayed as representing different races. In legend and folk tale they have received fictional names and all sorts of embellishments.

By comparison, Matthew's record is dull. He reports, 'some wise men from the east came to Jerusalem' (v. 1 CEV). On their arrival they asked the question, 'Where is the child born to be king of the Jews?' (v. 2) News of their quest reached the ears of King Herod. For him, intrigue was a way of life and no doubt he believed there was some ulterior motive behind their visit. After making enquiries about where the Christ was to be born, he arranged a private interview with them, then directed them to Bethlehem. There they found the child and after presenting their gifts to him, they 'returned to their country by another route' (v. 12), being warned in a dream not to report back to the king. When Herod discovered they had departed from the country without returning to him, he ordered the massacre of all baby boys in Bethlehem under the age of two years (v. 16).

 ## Noting the emotion

It is reported that Mary, when confronted by the angel was '**greatly troubled**' (Luke 1:29), the adverb 'greatly' suggesting she was close to **panic**. What does this indicate? Was her concern due to **fear** or **anxiety** as to the purpose of the angel's visit? She '**wondered** what kind of greeting this might be'. When Gabriel spells out the details, Mary is **puzzled**. 'How can this happen? I'm not married' (1:34 CEV). When God's purpose is explained, Mary **quietly accepts** this, 'May it be to me as you have said' (1:38).

Mary was engaged to Joseph, and in those times, this agreement was binding and a divorce was required to break it. Joseph's reaction was predictable. Matthew reports that on learning Mary was pregnant, Joseph 'decided to quietly call off the wedding' (Matthew 1:19 CEV). He does **not** seem to have been an **impetuous** person. He considered what to do about the situation, and while doing this, the angel brought him guidance 'in a dream' (v. 20). As a result of this, he had enough faith to go ahead with the wedding as planned, 'but they didn't sleep together before her baby was born' (v. 25 CEV).

The birth took place in Bethlehem, the 'home town' of King David's descendants (Luke 2:4 CEV). Joseph, a descendant of David had to return to his 'home town' with Mary, because the Romans had ordered a census in Palestine. Suitable accommodation would have been hard to find. Luke records that the birth occurred during their stay but it may not have occurred on the day they arrived – 'while they were there, the time came for the baby to be born' (v. 6).

Luke's attention then shifts to another incident, the angel's announcement to the shepherds. They reacted emotionally – in fact they were '**terrified**' (v. 9). Artists who depict this scene for children's books rarely capture this. Rather they show figures surprised or slinking back apprehensively, seldom depicting the shepherds as 'terrified'.

After reassurance by the angel, the shepherds witness the spectacle of the angelic choir, their fear changing to **excited anticipation**. They decide to follow the angel's directions and find the baby just as described to them. Later, as they return to the fields, their excitement begins to spill over, and they report what they have witnessed to all and sundry, who 'were **amazed** at what the shepherds said to them' (v. 18).

We don't know how much time elapsed between Jesus' birth and the visit of the Magi (wise men) but it is most unlikely that it was on the night of his birth as often depicted in books and Christmas pageants (see Matthew 2:11, cf. Luke 2:7). When these men arrived in Jerusalem they began asking around the streets and hotels about the whereabouts of one 'born to be king' (Matthew 2:2 CEV), causing considerable **consternation** to break out in the royal court. King Herod – a person not likely to foster the rise of any potential rival – was '**disturbed**' (Matthew 2:3). And if Herod was troubled, so too were the residents of Jerusalem, who knew from first hand experience that his reactions to possible threats could result in random reprisals that spelt trouble for them.

Herod's meeting with the Magi was arranged 'secretly'. He questioned them carefully as to the 'exact time the star had appeared' (Matthew 2:7). Having already questioned the 'chief priests and teachers of the law' for information relating to the birth of 'the Christ', Herod directed the Magi to Bethlehem (vv. 4-8).

Think about how he would have delivered his instructions – perhaps with an oily smile – **cynically** asking them to return with news of the baby's location so that he could go 'and worship him' (v. 8). His true attitude would later be revealed. When he realised that he had been 'outwitted' by the Magi when they failed to return to him after they achieved their goal, Herod was '**furious**, and he gave orders to kill all the boys in Bethlehem and its vicinity' who were two years old and under.' His **cruel** action caused great distress (vv. 16,18).

 ### Extra comment

In a radio interview given by the actress who played the leading role of a nun in the TV series *The Brides of Christ*, she described herself as a 'lapsed Catholic'. This came about through her doubts about 'the infallibility of the Pope and the virgin birth'. Many people struggle with the claim that Mary was a virgin at the time of her conception. Taking the record at face value, it is clear that Mary understood Gabriel to mean that she would bear a child without the intervention of a man. To us this seems impossible, yet we must recognise that the alternative is that Jesus had a human father. To accept this undermines the claim that Jesus is the Son of God.

For children

Most young children know that babies come out of their mummy's tummy and are not delivered by the stork or found in the cabbage patch as earlier generations were told. But for many young children, they do not know as yet the part their daddy played in this. Because children's understanding of sex is limited, the theological significance of Mary's virginity at the time of her conception is beyond the understanding of children in the infants and lower primary grades. For those working with older children and teenagers, this aspect will come under constant challenge. One way of dealing with this is to ask the question, 'If the account is a myth rather than history, why would such a story be invented?'

JESUS PRESENTED IN THE TEMPLE

 Focus Passage: Luke 2:21-40

This section introduces us to two beautiful people, Simeon and Anna.

Simeon is described as being both righteous and devout. Anna too is dedicated to God. She never left the Temple but 'worshipped night and day, fasting and praying' (v. 37). Both were rewarded for their faith and allowed to witness the arrival of the promised one, 'the Lord's Christ' (v. 26).

 Charting the action

The baby Jesus was eight days old when he was circumcised and officially named 'Jesus, the name the angel had given him before he had been conceived' (v. 21). Later, after the period of purification that followed childbirth, his parents travelled to Jerusalem to consecrate him in the Temple (v. 22).

Simeon was very much in tune with God for we read 'the Holy Spirit was upon him' (v. 25). It had been revealed to him that he would not die until he had seen the fulfilment of God's promise to send the Christ. At the precise time that Jesus was brought to the Temple by his parents, the Spirit prompted Simeon to enter there also.

As Simeon was rejoicing, the elderly prophet Anna, also present in the Temple, joined in the celebration.

 ## Noting the emotion

The most prominent emotion here is one of **patience rewarded**. Simeon was probably getting on in years and Anna is described as 'very old' (v. 36). Yet still they waited expectantly for the fulfilment of God's promises. I imagine there would have been tears of joy pouring down Simeon's wrinkled cheeks as he took the baby Jesus in his arms. His understanding of what this baby would become is directly attributed to the guidance of the Holy Spirit (v. 25).

Simeon burst out with spontaneous praise, to the surprise of the parents who **'marvelled'** at what he said (v. 33).

 ## Extra comment

Much of what Simeon had to say was prophetic. He warned Mary of the suffering she was to experience in the future, when 'a sword will pierce your own soul too' (v. 35).

THE BOY JESUS AT THE TEMPLE

 Focus Passages: *Luke 2:41-52*

This passage is unique. It is the only account we have of any event that occurred in the first thirty years of Jesus' life. This heightens its significance, for until Jesus began his active ministry, he was 'unnoticed and unknown'.

 Charting the action

The parents of Jesus visited Jerusalem annually for the Passover celebrations. When Jesus was twelve years of age they went up 'as usual' to participate (v. 41). They were part of a large group, so on the homeward journey, his absence from the party of returning pilgrims wasn't noticed until they had travelled for a whole day (v. 44). Returning to the city, his parents searched for him for three days. They finally discovered him in the Temple precincts with the teachers, 'listening to them and asking them questions' (v. 46). After what could only be described as a strained conversation, the family returned home to Nazareth.

 Noting the emotion

Imagine the conversation between Jesus' parents. It might have gone like this:

'Joseph, have you seen Jesus?'

'No, isn't he with you?'

'No! I haven't seen him since we left Jerusalem.'

'He's probably with some of our relatives or friends. I'll see if I can find him.'

A twelve-year-old boy does not need watching at every moment so it is quite feasible that his parents travelled a whole day before missing him. His absence was probably greeted with more **annoyance** than **anxiety** by his parents at first, but there was nothing for it but to turn back and search for him. After three days of searching they must have been greatly **distressed**, so when they finally discovered him in the Temple courts Mary's **irritation** is obvious. 'Son, why have you done this to us? Your father and I have been very **worried** and we've been searching for you!' (v. 48 CEV)

Any mother who has searched for and found an apparently unharmed and unconcerned lost child will sense something of her annoyance. In the face of her rebuke, Jesus expressed **astonishment** that his parents understood him so little. Surely the Temple should have been the first place to look for him. His reply contains Jesus' first recorded words: 'Didn't you know that I would be in my Father's house?' (v. 49 CEV). This brief sentence reveals an understanding of the special relationship Jesus had with God the Father. Mary had said 'your father and I', but Jesus referred to 'my Father'.

His reply **bewildered** his parents, but 'they did not understand what he was saying to them' (v. 50). Mary sensed that his reply had some significance as she 'treasured all these things in her heart' (v. 51). When Luke finally came to record the event for our benefit, this phrase suggests that Mary must have been his source of information.

 ### Extra comment

Commentators point out that the lack of information about the boyhood of Jesus is confirmation of the 'stamp of honest narrative'. What they mean by this is that if the account of Jesus' life were a fabrication, we would expect to find much more detail relating to his early years and perhaps some flashes of examples of supernatural power.

 ### For children

Teachers may like to focus on Jesus' submission to parental authority (v. 51).

JOHN THE BAPTIST PREPARES THE WAY

Focus Passages: *Luke 3:1-20*
John 1:19-34

When Paul White, the well-known author of the Jungle Doctor books was a young man, his attention was gripped by a startling headline in the local paper – 'Irish Evangelist calls Country Bishop, Stinking Polecat'. Thinking it would be entertaining to hear such a speaker, he attended the advertised meetings and through the preaching of the forthright Irishman, J.B. Nicholson, he was converted to Christianity. John the Baptist was a similar type of preacher.

 ## Charting the action

After the introductory chapter in Luke which gives details of his birth, we hear nothing more of John until he suddenly bursts into the spotlight with a challenging message. In it he urged people to repent and be baptised, to prepare for the coming of the Messiah.

John's message was stern and uncompromising. He was a preacher with no time for creature comforts. Dressed in rough homespun clothing made of camel's hair, he lived on a harsh diet of locusts and wild honey.

Picture him standing on the banks of the Jordan River looking contemptuously at the crowd milling forward in response to his preaching. Picture him too as he indicates to some of his followers the presence of Jesus, who happened to be passing by: 'Look, the Lamb of God, who takes away the sin of the world!' (John 1:29,35) John knew that this would result in the crowd transferring their loyalty to Jesus, yet he accepted this without flinching.

John knew that his was not the starring role. He illustrated this by contrasting the role of the groom at a wedding with that of the best man (John 3:29). 'Jesus must become more important, while I become less important' (John 3:30 CEV).

 Noting the emotion

To observe the emotions that John displayed, we need to range extensively over the early chapters of the gospels. These give us insight into John's character.

Undoubtedly he was **blunt**. Luke records that when people responded to his preaching, John was **sceptical** of their sincerity, describing them as a 'brood of vipers' (Luke 3:7). He challenged them to show evidence by their actions that their repentance was genuine. Perhaps he suspected that their desire to be baptised was just a fad.

He was a **wise** counsellor, able to give advice to a range of different people. Tax collectors were urged to be honest 'Don't make people pay more than they owe' (v. 13 CEV). Soldiers were instructed not to 'force people to pay money to make you leave them alone. Be satisfied with your pay' (v. 14 CEV).

So sound did his advice seem that the people 'became **excited** and **wondered**, "Could John be the Messiah?" ' (v. 15 CEV)

It is here that his **humility**, the strong point of John's character, comes to the fore. John knew his place and strongly affirmed that someone else, 'the thongs of whose sandals I am not worthy to untie' (v. 16) was coming.

He was **fearless** and didn't shrink from rebuking Herod, even though this led to his imprisonment (vv. 19,20) and subsequently, his death (Matthew 14:10).

Luke 7:26,28 records Jesus' opinion of John, 'A prophet? Yes ... more than a prophet.' 'Among those born of women there is no one greater than John'.

 Extra comment

In John 5:31-47, Jesus states that his sonship is based on a number of witnesses, one of whom is John. 'You have sent to

John and he has testified to the truth' (v. 33) In this passage he gives further insight into John's role, 'John was a lamp that burned and gave light, and you chose for a time to enjoy his light' (v. 35).

THE BAPTISM OF JESUS

 Focus Passages: Matthew 3:13-17
Luke 3:21-22
John 1:32-34

 ## Charting the action

John's ministry was marked by considerable success. As an indication of their repentance, crowds of people gathered at the Jordan River to be baptised by him. Jesus joined the throng and moved forward to be baptised along with the rest, but John questioned him as to the appropriateness of this action. Jesus encouraged John to go ahead and do his part.

As Jesus came up from the water, heaven opened and 'he saw the Spirit of God descending like a dove and lighting on him. And a voice from heaven said, "This is my Son, whom I love; with him I am well pleased"' (Matthew 3:16,17).

John's gospel gives us an interesting slant on this, reporting the incident from the Baptist's point of view. John the Baptist explains that 'the one who sent me to baptise with water ... told me, "You will see the Spirit come down and stay on someone"' (John 1:33 CEV). When this sign happened before his eyes, John was convinced that Jesus was the Son of God (v. 34).

 ## Noting the emotion

To a degree, we must read between the lines in this passage to sense the emotion of this moment, as the text gives us little direct indication of it. Undoubtedly John was **surprised** to discover Jesus amongst the group filing forward for baptism, for Matthew reports that John tried to deter him saying, I ought to be baptised by you. Why have you come to me?' (Matthew 3:14 CEV).

Jesus replied, 'For now, this is how it should be, because we must do all that God wants us to do' (v. 15 CEV), so John agreed to this.

 ### Extra comment

A voice from heaven spoke as Jesus was baptised saying, 'This is my own dear Son, and I am pleased with him' (v. 17 CEV). On another occasion, God's voice was heard again in miraculous fashion when Jesus chose Peter, James and John to accompany him up on the Mount of Transfiguration. There a voice made a similar statement to the earlier one, 'This is my chosen Son. Listen to what he says!' (Luke 9:35 CEV) Peter testified later to this experience, when he wrote in his second epistle, 'We were there with Jesus on the holy mountain and heard this voice speak from heaven' (2 Peter 1:18 CEV).

The third time the voice from heaven was heard came after Jesus' triumphal entry into Jerusalem (today called Palm Sunday) just a few days before the crucifixion. It said, 'I have already brought glory to myself, and I will do it again!' (John 12:28 CEV) On this occasion, 'when the crowd heard the voice, some of them thought it was thunder' (v. 29 CEV). Jesus explained to them that the voice spoke 'for your benefit, not mine' (v. 30).

This latter incident is included as it gives us some understanding of the emotions felt by people on hearing a supernatural voice. They were **puzzled** by the noise, and talked about it. This led them into an interesting dialogue with Jesus. Whether the noise made them afraid is not recorded.

THE TEMPTATION OF JESUS

 Focus Passages: *Matthew 4:1-11*
                             Luke 4:1-13

Don't you love the biblical puzzles that no one can solve? Matthew lists the second and third temptations in a different order to the way that Luke reports them, something the Tyndale commentary notes 'has never been satisfactorily explained'.

 ## Charting the action

If we follow Luke's account, Jesus was 'led by the Spirit' (v. 1) into the desert. During the forty days Jesus was there he fasted. The devil confronted him and sought to tempt him in three ways:

He suggested that Jesus satisfy his physical hunger by turning the stones of the desert into bread.

He offered Jesus unlimited power so long as Jesus was willing to worship him.

He suggested to Jesus that by performing a miraculous act – jumping off the pinnacle of the Temple – this would provide a shortcut to his claim to be the Son of God in gaining general acceptance.

In each case Jesus defended himself, countering the temptations by referring to the Scriptures.

 ## Noting the emotion

Anyone who has been without food for a length of time will appreciate how **lethargic** and **depressed** you become. After forty days of fasting Jesus would have been very **vulnerable** and it was at this point, when his resistance was at its lowest, that the devil suggested an easy solution to his hunger: 'If you are God's Son, tell this stone to turn into bread' (Luke 4:3 CEV). He invited Jesus to satisfy his physical need through appealing to the appetites.

The temptation is meant to create **doubt** in Jesus' mind: 'If you are God's Son'. Notice that these same words were flung at him three years later by people in the crowd, as he hung upon the cross – 'Come down from the cross, if you are the Son of God' (Matthew 27:40).

In his reply, Jesus quoted Deuteronomy 8:3 where Moses is urging the people to remember how they were led in the times of their desert wandering. There they faced hunger but in the process learned that provision of our physical needs was not the most important thing in life.

The second temptation is also answered with a quote from Deuteronomy, this time from chapter 6, verse 13.

On the third occasion the devil tried to **cloud the issue**, quoting from Psalm 91:11. He quoted from Scripture to assure Jesus that if he launched himself from the Temple pinnacle, he would be safe. It was a wrong use of Scripture. To **defend** himself, Jesus again used a quote from Deuteronomy, chapter 6, verse 16.

Commentators point out that when you read Jesus' reply in the original language, it is **strong** and **expressive**, 'You shall not tempt to the extreme the Lord your God' (Luke 4:12).

Jesus knew that he should not presume on all that God was able to do nor ask God to intervene to save him miraculously if he did something foolish. When Luke concluded this episode with the words, 'the devil ... left him until an opportune time' (4:13) this did not mean that Jesus was no longer subject to further temptation. For Jesus as for us, 'There is no freedom from temptation in this life'.

JESUS REJECTED AT NAZARETH

Focus Passage: *Luke 4:14-30*
Other references: *Isaiah 61:1-2*
Luke 4:1-14
Luke 7:19-22

Charting the action

Early in his ministry Jesus returned to his home town of Nazareth after a period spent teaching in synagogues throughout the region of Galilee. Although Luke doesn't mention them directly, instances of healing apparently accompanied his preaching. Now the people of Nazareth were hoping for similar demonstrations of his power that 'we have heard that you did in Capernaum' (v. 23).

When Jesus attended the synagogue on the Sabbath, he was invited to read from the prophet Isaiah. Selecting chapter 61, he read the first couple of paragraphs then stopped abruptly, returned the scroll to the attendant and sat down. Stopping part way through a sentence caught everyone by surprise and when he announced that the passage they had heard was now being fulfilled, tongues began to wag. At first his remarks were received congenially (v. 22) but as he continued, the mood of the people in the synagogue turned to rage and they attempted to lynch him. But Jesus just passed through the crowd, emerging unharmed.

Noting the emotion

The frequent references to various emotions in this report are striking. Imagine the electrifying effect that Jesus, by stopping part way through the familiar reading, would have on the synagogue congregation. Luke reports that 'the eyes of everyone ... were fastened on him' (v. 20). They were so **startled** that they gave him their rapt attention.

'Today', he announced, 'this scripture is fulfilled in your hearing' (v. 21) How **puzzling** to those present – Jesus was a local boy, Joseph's son, 'all spoke well of him' – yet here was Jesus, appearing to apply Isaiah's prophecy to himself. They 'were **amazed**' at this (v. 22). When he made further statements, their mood changed dramatically. To prove his point that 'no prophet is accepted in his home-town' (v. 24), he used two illustrations from their history. The first related to the widow of Zarephath (1 Kings 17) and the second to Naaman the Syrian (2 Kings 5). Behind these stories were two issues that were causing much **dissension** at the time: One concerned the breaking of the Sabbath rules, the other the suggestion that the Lord could look favourably upon foreigners (Gentiles). Both examples that Jesus used related to foreigners, enough to stir the emotions of those present to white hot intensity. Hearing him mention them made the townspeople **furious**. Picture the turmoil that followed, as former neighbours 'drove him out of town' (v. 29), intending to kill him. And yet, finding himself in this terrible situation following their drastic reaction to his comments, Jesus **calmly** 'walked right through the crowd and went on his way' (v. 30).

 For children

There is scope for both expression and gesture by the storyteller in this incident. Keep in mind that prophets and prophecies will most likely be beyond the experience of children so they will need explanation. Similarly, do not assume that the children know the Old Testament incidents Jesus refers to, so weave some of the details into your narrative. Luke 7:19-22 is a useful link for expanding this account. When Jesus replied to John the Baptist's message to him, John being familiar with Isaiah's words, would have recognised the link Jesus was making.

Extra comment

An examination of Isaiah 61 will reveal that Jesus omitted the phrase, 'the day of vengeance of our God', a day still in the future. Luke 4:30 does not suggest a miracle, but rather something about the presence of Jesus, which made enemies and a rioting crowd succumb to his calm bearing, enabling him to step quietly through them, free and unharmed.

What sort of person are we dealing with here?

Alternative methods of presentation
Try telling the story in the first person from the viewpoint of the synagogue attendant. Or perhaps a reporter from the *Jerusalem Herald* could interview a member of the crowd, seeking an explanation of what they had witnessed and the ensuing uproar.

JESUS CHANGES WATER INTO WINE

 Focus Passage: *John 2:1-11*

We have no knowledge of how much wine the family provided for this wedding but when this ran out, a staggering quantity of wine was made available to the guests, through the miraculous intervention of Jesus. According to John's report, the capacity of each of these six stone water jars was eighty to one hundred litres (v. 6). The master of ceremonies could not get over the quality of the wine served to the guests after the initial festivities. Wow! It must have been some wedding – every relative and friend of the couple must have rolled up to help them celebrate. Guests had already 'had plenty' (v. 10 CEV) of wine and now a further five to six hundred litres awaited consumption. Either the crowd was extensive or there were some heavy drinkers amongst them!

Charting the action

Mary, the mother of Jesus was a guest at this village wedding celebration as was Jesus and his disciples. The function flowed along smoothly until the wine ran out. Sympathising with their host's predicament, Mary drew Jesus' attention to the problem implying, 'Can't you help them out?' Jesus' reply suggests he wasn't keen but Mary was undeterred and ordered the servants to do whatever Jesus instructed.

Six stone water jars were then filled to the brim and the servants told to draw water from them and carry it to the Master of Ceremonies.

 Noting the emotion

There are no direct references to emotion in this record so it is necessary to think about the people involved and to sense their reactions.

The first emotion would have been one of **consternation**. How **embarrassing** for the family, when they ran out of wine in the middle of the party.

We can only speculate how Mary knew that Jesus could solve their predicament – until this moment Jesus had performed no miracles. He seemed reluctant to act when Mary approached him, 'Mother, my time hasn't yet come! You mustn't tell me what to do' (v. 4 CEV).

There is an 'upstairs, downstairs' aspect to this story. The man in charge didn't know where the extra wine had come from, 'but the servants did' (v. 9 CEV). Perhaps they grinned secretly to themselves, seeing the fuss made about something they knew to be only water.

The Master of Ceremonies was effusive, commending the bridegroom for keeping the best wine till last.

John stated what resulted from this event: 'He thus revealed his glory, and his disciples put their faith in him' (v. 11).

JESUS DRIVES OUT
AN EVIL SPIRIT

 Focus Passage: *Luke 4:31-37*

'Hey, Jesus of Nazareth, what do you want with us?' (v. 34 CEV)

The shouting of the demon possessed man shatters a tranquil setting.

 ## Charting the action

While teaching in the synagogue on the Sabbath during a visit to Capernaum, Jesus was interrupted by a man who began to verbally abuse him. The words came from the man's mouth but it was a demon speaking. The significant thing about the demon's challenge was that he identified 'Jesus of Nazareth' as 'the Holy One of God' (v. 34). Jesus immediately ordered him to be quiet and to come out of the man. During the violent departure, the man was thrown to the ground in front of everyone, but survived unharmed.

 ## Noting the emotion

'His teaching **amazed** them because he spoke with power' (v. 32 CEV). In those days, when 'books' (scrolls) were few and most learning came through oral tradition, teaching largely consisted of memorising large chunks of the Bible or its commentators, with the rabbis repeating word for word what had been passed on to them. Comments were traced back to the originator of the saying through a named chain of people. Originality and comment was most unusual. Here, to the amazement of the synagogue congregation, Jesus, a local tradesman, appeared to be stating his own opinion, with obvious authority.

This incident in Luke agrees with Mark's account of Jesus healing people who were demon possessed. 'The demons knew who he was, and he didn't let them speak' (Mark 1:34 CEV). Jesus' claims were not based on the testimony of demons.

His power **amazed** them. 'All the people were **amazed** and said to each other, "What is this teaching? With authority and power he gives orders to evil spirits and they come out!"' (Luke 4:36)

This incident was not an isolated event and other reports of his power over demonic forces were circulating. Tongues wagged: 'News about him spread throughout the surrounding area' (v. 37).

 For children

In western communities, those who teach younger children are wise to avoid stories of demons, as incidents of this type are difficult to explain.

THE CALLING OF THE FIRST DISCIPLES

 Focus Passage: Luke 5:1-11

'Caught anything?'

'Nah! Only a couple of **minnows!**'

Even though the passing stranger is only making conversation we would all be happier if we could display a nice **bream** to reveal our skill.

 Charting the action

Peter and his partners James and John, were commercial fishermen and like all those who make a living from fishing, would be experts in local fish lore. But on this occasion, despite their skill, after working hard all night at throwing their nets and repeatedly hauling them in, the nets still came up empty. When Peter tried again at Jesus' suggestion, the catch of fish was so extensive that the nets were in danger of breaking. They had to call for help from their 'partners in the other boat' (v. 7). As a result of this, they left their boats and followed Jesus.

 ### Noting the emotion

Jesus had been sitting in Simon Peter's boat teaching a large number of people eager to hear him. 'They crowded around him' (v. 1 CEV). At the conclusion of his discourse he suggested to Peter that he 'Row the boat out into the deep water and let your nets down to catch some fish' (v. 4 CEV). Peter was **less than enthusiastic**, even **pessimistic**: 'We've worked hard all night long and haven't caught a thing. But if you tell me to, I will let the nets down' (v. 5 CEV).

Visualise what followed. The nets thrown, then hauled in, straining to such an extent that they were in danger of breaking. Imagine Peter surrounded by a mass of wriggling, flapping, struggling fish – legs bracing, arm muscles bulging from the strain of heaving on that tremendous weight.

Initially he would have shouted from sheer **excitement** but soon his shouts would change to **panic** as he screamed out to his partners in the other boat for help.

Imagine them excitedly throwing fish into the other boat, anxiety etched on their faces, with both boats becoming so overloaded that they were in danger of sinking. The realisation of what this catch signified must have flooded into Peter's mind. Fearfully he knelt down and spoke to Jesus, as filled with awe, he realised he was in the presence of the divine: 'Lord, don't come near me! I'm a sinner' (v. 8 CEV).

All those present were '**astonished** at the catch of fish they had taken' (v. 9).

Peter's reaction to the huge catch was to recognise the divine in it and, without hesitation, he left his boats to become one of Jesus' followers.

Extra comment

The memory of this miracle never left the disciples. When it recurred a second time three years later, John immediately recognised the significance of what was happening. 'It is the Lord!' he told Peter eagerly (John 21:7).

 For children

The storyteller will have no difficulty in capturing the interest of the class because this exciting incident has such graphic action. It can be linked with the story of the calming of the storm in Luke 8, another occasion where Jesus demonstrated his power over nature.

THE CALL OF NATHANAEL

 Focus Passage: John 1:43-51

Have you ever tried to tell a friend about Jesus? Not easy is it? Hang in there, for Philip tried, with surprising results.

 Charting the action

The record says little. Nathanael is seen sitting under a fig tree, probably meditating, when Philip approaches him with news of Jesus.

Philip persuades his friend to come and meet Jesus and as a result, Nathanael becomes one of Jesus' intimate followers.

 Noting the emotion

While there is little action there is plenty of emotion to report.

Nathanael was probably quite **relaxed** and peaceful until his tranquility was shattered by Philip's eager babble. Philip was **bursting** with exciting news.

'We have found the one that Moses and the Prophets wrote about. He is Jesus, the son of Joseph from Nazareth' (1:45 CEV).

His friend's reaction was far from enthusiastic.

'Nazareth!' he **sneered** 'Can anything good come from there?' (v. 46)

Philip wasn't discouraged by the tone of derision in Nathanael's voice. 'Come and see', was his simple appeal.

Such was the basis of their friendship that despite his **scepticism**, Nathanael agreed to accompany Philip.

'Here is a true Israelite, in whom there is nothing false.' (v. 47) Nathanael must have been close enough to overhear this remark by Jesus, for he blurted out in **astonishment,** 'How do you know me?' (v. 48) When Jesus replied that he had seen him while he was under the fig tree before Philip called him, Nathanael was **overwhelmed** and made a remarkable response:

'Rabbi, you are the Son of God and the King of Israel!' (v. 49 CEV)

 ### Extra comment

It is significant to compare Philip's description of Jesus, 'Jesus of Nazareth, the son of Joseph' (v. 45) with Nathanael's declaration, 'You are the Son of God and the King of Israel'. Nathanael took a giant stride beyond Philip's understanding of who Jesus was.

 ### For children

A number of people I have met have told me that they were first introduced to Jesus by a mate at school. Providing their instruction in witnessing is done sensibly, even children can be encouraged to pass on the good news.

A MAN WITH LEPROSY

 Focus Passage: Mark 1:40-45
Other references: Matthew 8:1-4
Luke 5:12-16

 ## Charting the action

A man with leprosy came to Jesus pleading for healing and Jesus responded immediately. Jesus reached out his hand and touched him saying, 'I am willing. Be clean!' (Mark 1: 41) He then sent the man away, instructing him to keep quiet about what happened. The man ignored this request, thus hindering his work, so 'Jesus could no longer enter a town openly but stayed outside in lonely places' (v. 45).

 ## Noting the emotion

The man came and 'begged him on his knees' (v. 40), the action indicating his emotion. He was **desperate** so he begged. This act of falling 'on his knees', an act of homage to a king, suggests '**humility**'.

Despite the leper's confidence that Jesus could heal him, he expresses doubt that Jesus would be willing to do this. But Jesus knew how much this man had **suffered**, not only from the disfiguring disease, but also from the ostracism that all lepers endured.

Mark reports that Jesus was 'filled with **compassion**' (v. 41) at the sight of this unfortunate man, and reached out and touched him.

Imagine the **shock** the leper received – trembling at being touched by a non-leper. It was probably years since he had last felt the touch of a 'clean' hand.

But what follows indicates considerable tension: 'Jesus sent him away at once with a **strong warning**' (v. 43).

Bible commentaries suggest a variety of reasons for why Jesus demanded that the man keep the matter to himself.

Jesus frequently directed those he healed to do this and mostly it was ignored.

The most obvious reason for asking the man to remain silent was to prevent the incident from becoming public as it would hinder Jesus' ministry if it became known he had touched a leper. Touching a leper made him ceremonially unclean. As Jesus found it necessary to avoid the towns for a period, this would appear to be the case.

 ## Extra comment

So why did the restored leper ignore the stern warning he had been given and begin 'to talk freely, spreading the news'? (v. 45) It is difficult for us to appreciate the situation of lepers in those days. Segregated from the community and their immediate family, they were forced to carry warning bells and shout 'unclean, unclean' whenever they came within earshot of other people. Unable to work, they existed on handouts and whatever they could scavenge.

They were considered the lowest of the low – outcast, despised, shunned and abused because the general population feared contamination by them. Is it any wonder that this man ignored the restraints placed on him just so he could reach the one he expected would be able to heal him?

 ## For children

I don't use this story with children, preferring the greater detail of the incident of the ten lepers who were healed. (See p. 103)

THE CALL OF MATTHEW

Focus Passage: Matthew 9:9-12
Other references: Mark 2:13-17
                    Luke 5:27-31

Throughout the history of occupied peoples, the general population has always despised citizens who collaborate with the conquerors. During the Roman occupation of Palestine, Jews directed their hatred at those who served as tax collectors.

 ### Charting the action

When Jesus passed by and issued his invitation to 'Follow me', Matthew was busy in his tax collector's booth. Without hesitation, Matthew did so. This contact introduced Jesus to a number of other tax collectors and 'sinners' who gathered in Matthew's house for a meal. Luke describes the occasion as 'a great banquet'.

 ### Noting the emotion

We cannot tell what Matthew thought when Jesus called him to follow, as the record gives no direct indication of his emotion. His response is so prompt that we must wonder if he had some previous contact with Jesus. Matthew sets us all a good example, rounding up his friends and inviting them to come to a meal to meet Jesus. Naturally, many of his friends were also tax collectors, and Jesus' willingness to associate with them brought scathing criticism from the Pharisees, the religious leaders of the day.

Their question was addressed to Jesus' disciples, 'Why does your teacher eat with tax collectors and "sinners"?' (v. 11)

Overhearing their question, Jesus chose to answer it himself, 'It is not the healthy who need a doctor, but the sick' (v. 12). Jesus went on to explain that he had not come to minister to the self-righteous, but to those aware of their need. He referred them to a passage in the Old Testament (Hosea 6:6), 'Go and learn what this means: "I desire mercy, not sacrifice".' This sums up what God finds pleasing.

The thought could never have occurred to the Pharisees that God might find it more pleasing to see them mingling with sinners in an effort to win them, rather than their efforts to live separately from people they considered spiritually inferior, to avoid being contaminated by them. Jesus wanted them to grasp the idea that for him to refuse to associate with the disreputable was as absurd as a doctor refusing to have anything to do with the sick.

But no sooner had this interruption to the meal been dealt with than another one occurred, a complaint from the disciples of John the Baptist. Poor Matthew, it wasn't his day!

John was living an alternative lifestyle, opting out of everyday society and living a life of stern discipline. His camel hair coat wasn't designed for comfort and his diet of locusts and wild honey could never be described as 'living it up!' John urged his followers to adopt a similar ascetic lifestyle. 'The man with two tunics should share with him who has none, and the one who has food should do the same' (Luke 3:11). Some of John's disciples must have observed Jesus and his disciples enjoying the lavish fare provided by the wealthy tax collector, which contrasted starkly with their own way of life. What prompted them to approach Jesus with the question, 'Why do we and the Pharisees often go without eating, while your disciples never do?' (Matthew 9:14 CEV) Was it **jealousy** or **self-righteousness**?

In his reply, Jesus uses the image of a bridegroom, which John himself had used when speaking about Jesus (John 3:27-30). The wedding guests cannot be expected to fast while the bridegroom is still with them. Later on 'the bridegroom will be taken from them; then they will fast' (Matthew 9:15).

This is probably the first public hint of the violent end Jesus knew awaited him.

Extra comment

When I first became a Christian I was given a Bible and urged to read it. Knowing nothing of Bible reading systems and helps like Scripture Union, I started at the beginning of Matthew, making notes as I went. I can remember being completely bewildered by Matthew 9:16-17, about cloth and wineskins. Try as I might, I could make no sense of these verses.

John's disciples fasted for reasons linked to the past. But what Jesus is indicating here through his reference to new cloth and new wine, is that he had come to introduce an entirely new way of life and not merely to patch up the old religion. Jesus knew that those trained in the tradition of the Pharisees or practising a rigid discipline like the disciples of John, would find it hard to accept new truths. 'No one wants new wine after drinking old wine. They say, "the old wine is better"' (Luke 5:39 CEV).

Jesus knew that his teaching would be unpalatable to some. Their prejudices would be so strong that they would not even try the new.

JESUS CHASES THE TRADERS FROM THE TEMPLE

 Focus Passage: John 2:12-25

 Charting the action

It seems to me that Jesus' attack on the Temple traders was premeditated. Observing what they were doing, he took the time to make a whip out of cords before stamping in to create chaos by opening the pens of livestock, tipping over the money changers' tables, ordering the dove sellers to take their birds away.

The Jews challenged him to show his authority for doing this.

 Noting the emotion

Although this action was planned rather than a spur of the moment reaction, nevertheless something about the **vehemence** of his action prevented anyone from attempting to thwart him.

'Then the Jews demanded of him. "What miraculous sign can you show us to prove your authority to do all this?"' (v. 18)

They **demanded** a sign and he countered this by offering them the biggest sign of all: 'Destroy this temple, and I will raise it again in three days' (v. 19).

They had no idea what he was talking about. Thinking he was referring to the huge building that surrounded them, their reply, 'It has taken forty-six years to build this temple and you are going to raise it in three days?' probably was accompanied by much raucous laughter (v. 20).

In an aside, John explains for the benefit of his readers that Jesus was speaking about his body, though at the time the disciples were just as bewildered about his meaning as were his enemies (v. 22). And, although his statement was incomprehensible to them, his enemies continued to puzzle over it. During Jesus' trial, two of them recalled his words and reported to Caiaphas, 'This fellow said, "I am able to destroy the temple of God and rebuild it in three days"' (Matthew 26:61).

Later, when Jesus was on the cross, he was taunted with, 'So! You who are going to destroy the temple and build it in three days, come down from the cross and save yourself!' (Mark 15:29,30)

On the day after the crucifixion a delegation came to Pilate saying, 'Sir, we remember that while he was still alive that deceiver said, "After three days I will rise again"'

(Matthew 27:63). They had finally worked it out. As there is no record that Jesus ever said this publicly, they must have been referring to this statement.

JESUS HEALS THE PARALYTIC

 Focus Passage: *Mark 2:1-12*

Some sermons stick in your mind, probably due to their structure. One I recall on this incident made three points: 'Those that helped, those that hindered and he who heals.'

 ## Charting the action

Four people helped, carrying the paralysed man down the road to the house where Jesus was at home. When they encountered their first difficulty, these four determined men weren't daunted. Finding the crowd packed around the door, preventing them from reaching their objective, they used their initiative to make a hole in the roof and lowered their friend into the room that way.

Seeing their faith, Jesus declared that the man's sins were forgiven. After dealing with the unspoken criticism of some teachers of the law who were 'sitting there' (v. 6; were they first in, or were they given seats because of their importance?) Jesus instructed the paralysed man to take up his bed and walk. He complied with this directive, pushing his way out carrying his bed, to the astonishment of the crowd.

 ## Noting the emotion

As Mark does not record the emotions of either the paralytic or his friends, we must try to think our way into the situation to get the feel of their reactions. What was the reaction of the man when his friends burst in to tell him of their plan to take him to Jesus? How would the men feel when they arrived to discover the house full of people and many more packed around the door? What was their reaction when one of them suggested the crazy idea of breaking in through the roof? What were their thoughts on hearing Jesus say to their friend 'Son, your sins are forgiven'? (v. 5)

We can only speculate on what might have been the feelings of the teachers of the law, who Mark suggests were thinking, 'Why would he say such a thing? He must think he is God! Only God can forgive sins' (v. 6 CEV). Jesus sensed their unspoken **criticism** and immediately brought it out into the open, **challenging** it:

'Is it easier for me to tell this crippled man that his sins are forgiven or to tell him to get up and pick up his mat and go on home? I will show you that the Son of Man has the right to forgive sins here on earth' (vv. 9-10 CEV). When the crippled man picked up his mat and pushed his way out of the room at Jesus' order, the crowd was **stunned**.

Picture the look on their faces as they gasp, 'We have never seen anything like this!' (v. 12) The faith of the man's friends was rewarded. They must have jumped for **joy** as they clambered down from the roof to accompany him home.

 Extra comment

When Jesus asked which was the easier, to announce that the man's sins were forgiven or to tell him to take up his mat and walk, he was responding to the teachers of the law's unspoken question, 'Who can forgive sins but God only?' Their question was a fair one, for Jesus' ability to heal demonstrated divine power. To forgive sins or make a crippled man walk is impossible for ordinary mortals. Jesus is laying out the evidence for all to see, displaying his claim to be divine.

 For children

The following outline uses the bed as the focal point:

- Speak about the pleasure of tucking into a nice warm bed on a winter's night.
- Introduce the man whose bed was his prison and explain his problem.
- Describe his friends carrying him on his bed to the house where Jesus was staying and their frustration in not being able to get in.
- Explain how they solved their problem by lowering his bed down through the roof.
- Report the conversation that followed, and its implication.
- Focus on Jesus' instruction to the man to 'pick up his bed' and describe the astonishment of the people when he is able to do so.
- Conclude by referring to the man's bedtime that night, when he would get into his bed knowing that it was no longer his prison.
- The man had been given more than a new set of legs. He had been forgiven. Jesus had healed his heart as well.

When I have questioned groups of children familiar with this incident, I have discovered that those who have taught them have emphasised the miraculous healing, ignoring or avoiding the fact that the Lord declared the man's sins forgiven. This incident gives an opportunity to teach children about sin and forgiveness – *don't miss it.*

THE VISIT OF NICODEMUS

   Focus Passage: *John 3:1-21*

This chapter has probably been the basis of more sermons than any other chapter in the New Testament because it contains the verse described as 'the gospel in a nutshell', John 3:16. But despite its popularity, it is not an easy passage to explain.

Charting the action

The report records a conversation between Nicodemus and Jesus, but apart from the explanation that Nicodemus came 'at night' there is no action.

Nicodemus most likely chose to come at night so as to keep his visit private, but it could also be because he was a busy man and at night he could hold an unhurried conversation with Jesus.

 Noting the emotion

Nicodemus' opening gambit is non-committal: 'Sir, we know that God has sent you to teach us. You couldn't work these miracles, unless God was with you' (v. 2 CEV). His statement reveals that he has received news of Jesus' prowess in performing miracles.

When his polite greeting was brushed aside with Jesus' blunt response, 'I tell you the truth, no one can see the kingdom of God unless he is born again' (v. 3), Nicodemus must have received a **shock**. He takes this statement at face value, understanding it in a physical sense, and thus pointing out its absurdity: 'How can a man be born when he is old? Surely he cannot enter a second time into his mother's womb to be born!' (v. 4)

In reply, Jesus gives a slightly fuller explanation of the term 'born again' – 'No one can enter the kingdom of God unless he is born of water and the Spirit' (v. 5). But it appears that Nicodemus isn't much the wiser for this. So what did Jesus mean?

Commentators give a variety of explanations. One suggests that 'born of water' refers to physical birth, i.e. born out of water, and 'spirit' refers to spiritual birth. Another suggests that 'born of water' referred to John's baptism, which stood for repentance. 'From there the extension may be made to Christian baptism, which in its turn must be linked with the internal experience of new life in the Spirit.'

(Robin Nixon, *John*, Bible Study Books, Scripture Union, London, 1968) This isn't an easy jump to make, as Christian baptism seems to have a different emphasis to John's.

Another view is that 'water' refers to washing or cleansing and 'spirit' indicates the kind of cleansing Jesus meant, namely spiritual cleansing (see Titus 3:5). This spiritual cleansing comes only by birth 'from above' and is indispensable to our entrance into the kingdom of God.

Nicodemus' reaction to this is one of sheer **astonishment**. 'How can this be?' he asks. It is Jesus' turn to be **surprised**. 'You are Israel's teacher and you do not understand these things?' (v. 10)

The revelation that the new birth is the gateway to the Kingdom becomes a revelation about Jesus himself. 'No one has ever gone into heaven except the one who came down from heaven – the Son of Man' (v. 13). Jesus then indicates the unique significance of his death, using the analogy of the snake plague that distressed the Israelites on their journey in the desert. There God provided the cure for snakebite through Moses – any person bitten by a snake was cured if they looked at the bronze snake Moses held up on the pole (Numbers 21:4-9). Here Jesus tells Nicodemus something that he was not able to understand until later – that to obtain entry to eternal life you had to believe in Jesus' death upon the cross.

 Extra comment

Commentators suggest that verses 16-21 were not part of the conversation between the two men but were linked later by John when he compiled his gospel.

John later in his record gives us two other glimpses of Nicodemus:

He protests to the Jewish Council when it is proposed to condemn Jesus without giving him opportunity to defend himself (John 7:50,51).

In John 19:39, Nicodemus assists Joseph of Arimathea to bury the body of Jesus. John reports that he provided a mixture of myrrh and aloes weighing about seventy-five pounds (thirty-four kilograms). That amount must have been costly. To provide this is revealing, the action of someone devoted to Jesus. It would seem that Nicodemus was now prepared to be open about his faith in who Jesus was.

MEETING WITH THE SAMARITAN WOMAN

 Focus Passage: *John 4:1-42*

 ## Charting the action

Again dialogue between two people is reported.

Jesus was travelling through Samaritan territory, where normally Jewish travellers would take a longer route, to avoid contact with the Samaritans whom they despised.

Tired from the journey, Jesus sat by a well while his disciples went to the nearby town to purchase food. The time of day is significant. When the woman arrived to draw water, it was about the sixth hour, midday by our reckoning. We assume she came at that unlikely time to avoid contact with other people.

To her surprise she found a man sitting there. They conversed until interrupted by the return of the disciples.

The woman then left her water pot and hurried back to town to tell the people there of her experience and to urge them to come to meet Jesus. As a result, Jesus stayed with them for two days before moving on.

 ## Noting the emotion

In studying the conversation between the woman and Jesus much depends on how we interpret their dialogue.

The woman was **astonished** when the stranger lounging by the well spoke to her. Having already noticed he was Jewish, she expected him to ignore her. Instead he asked, 'Will you give me a drink?' (v. 7)

'*You* are a Jew and *I* am a Samaritan woman. How can *you* ask *me* for a drink?' (v. 9) By stressing the personal pronouns, this gives her words the inflection needed.

As the conversation progresses, it is obvious that Jesus is speaking in spiritual terms, while the woman thinks only of the physical and the actual.

'You have nothing to draw with and the well is deep. Where can you get this living water?' (v. 11) Again Jesus' reply focuses on the spiritual. Her reply seems cheeky, 'Sir, give me this water so that I won't get thirsty and have to keep coming here to draw water' (v. 15). As she is not treating his remarks seriously, he switches the conversation, saying abruptly, 'Go, call your husband and come back.' Her brief reply, 'I have no husband', seems to indicate a **defensiveness** on her part. (vv. 16,17) 'That's right,' Jesus replied, 'You're telling the truth. You don't have a husband. You have already been married five times, and the man you are now living with is not your husband' (v. 17 CEV).

What an incredible **shock** to discover that Jesus knew so much about her. So what did she do? She did what so many of us do when embarrassed, she changed the subject, referring to a long standing controversy, the preference of one location over another for the most suitable place to worship God.

With the conversation progressing along this line, Jesus revealed to her that he was the expected one, the Messiah, the Christ. 'I am that one, and I am speaking to you now' (v. 26 CEV). Why was Jesus so explicit? It probably resulted from the first sign of change in the woman's attitude, her recognition of Jesus as a prophet. His open declaration to her seems to be the natural consequence of her developing insight and her statement that when the Messiah comes, 'he'll explain everything to us' (v. 25).

The return of the disciples interrupted their conversation. They registered **surprise** that he was speaking to her. The woman, bursting with the news of her discovery hurried back to town. But now, instead of avoiding people, she openly approached people urging them to come to meet Jesus. 'Come and see a man who told me everything I've ever done! Could he be the Messiah?' (v. 28 CEV) Her **enthusiasm** was catching. 'Everyone in town went out to see Jesus.'

The incident has a fitting climax. The people of the town say to the woman, 'We've heard him ourselves, and we're certain that he is the Saviour of the world' (v. 42 CEV).

The title, 'Saviour of the world', is only used in one other place in the New Testament, in 1 John 4:14. It is most significant that it was Samaritans who first applied this title to Jesus.

 Extra comment

The Samaritans were a half-caste people bred from the remnant left behind in Samaria when it fell in 722 BC. Most of its people were exiled, and foreigners were imported there by the Assyrian conquerors. Jesus' attitude towards these despised people was very different from that of the Jews of his day. Not only did he openly mix with them on this occasion, he made a Samaritan the hero of one of his parables. In his final instruction to his disciples in Acts 1:8, Jesus included Samaria as one of the destinations for the preaching of the gospel.

 For children

This is not an easy story to use with children, due to the abstract nature of the discussion about 'living water'.

If the story is used, bear in mind that many children will come from homes where there are many different kinds of marital arrangements. In speaking about the woman's situation, it is best to simply state it and leave it at that, rather than attempt an explanation.

JESUS HEALS THE OFFICIAL'S SON

 Focus Passage: John 4:43-54

'What time is it?' To a degree, most of our lives are dominated by time. Often we ask the question as a casual enquiry, but in some circumstances the answer may cause us considerable anxiety.

In this story the timing of the event is especially relevant.

 ## Charting the action

When Jesus was on a visit to Cana, a 'certain royal official', a resident of Capernaum approached him (v. 46). Cana, John reminds us, was where Jesus turned water into wine. The official asked Jesus to heal his son, who was 'close to death' (v. 47).

At first Jesus appeared to fob him off but the official persisted. Jesus then told him to go, after telling him his son would live. The man took Jesus at his word and left but it is unclear as to why it took him until the next day to reach home. When given the news that his son had recovered, he enquired as to the time the recovery had occurred. Learning that it was at the exact time that Jesus had spoken 'he and all his household believed' (v. 53).

 ## Noting the emotion

This father was **desperate**. His son was 'close to death' and when he heard that Jesus was also visiting Cana he hurried to him and '**begged** him to come and heal his son'. Jesus' first response must have been off-putting to the official, 'You won't have faith unless you see miracles and wonders' (v. 48 CEV). Tenaciously the man continued his desperate appeal 'Lord, please come before my son dies!' (v. 49 CEV)

'Your son will live. Go back home to him' (v. 50 CEV). I imagine the father pausing while the implications of what Jesus had said sank in, coming to grips with the realisation that it was unnecessary for Jesus to physically come in contact with his son. He displayed incredible faith, for he 'took Jesus at his word and departed' (v. 50 CEV).

The biblical account says, 'while he was still on the way, his servants met him' (v. 51 CEV). What is puzzling is why it took him so long. Commentators estimate that the journey from Cana to Capernaum would have taken about five hours. The seventh hour (1.00 pm) should have given him ample time to reach home. Did he have business to attend to or did he wait to journey with others? We cannot know but what is obvious is that his faith was such that he didn't rush home anxiously, to check whether Jesus' word had been effective.

His servants and the family must have been **excited** for the servants didn't wait for him to return but met him along the road, bursting with the news that his son had recovered. 'What time did it happen?' he enquired. 'The fever left him yesterday at one o'clock' (v. 52 CEV). This was the exact time that Jesus said, 'your son will live'. We only have the simple statement that the man and everyone in his family became believers, but imagine the scene, with the official excitedly telling them his side of what had happened, persuading them that Jesus must be the Messiah as only the Messiah could effect such a miraculous cure.

 Extra comment

What would Herod have thought had he known that an official in his own court was a believer in Jesus?

 For children

You could tell this incident from the viewpoint of the official's wife. Start by describing her **distress** when their son became ill. She could then tell of her **delight** when the son recovered and her **amazement** as her husband explained the reason for the recovery.

Then cross check the note on faith under the section on the woman who touched Jesus' coat, p. 76.

JESUS CALMS THE STORM

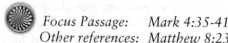

Focus Passage: *Mark 4:35-41*
Other references: *Matthew 8:23-27*
                   Luke 8:22-25

Many of us would have experienced an alarming incident in a boat or seen television coverage of some such event.

Once when crossing Lake Macquarie (near Newcastle, NSW) with friends, we developed engine trouble and were forced to beach our boat. As we struggled to drag it out of the reach of the pounding surf, an old lady appeared through the mist and sleet. 'You fellers are gamer than Ned Kelly', she said. 'There were three fishing boats swamped out there near the point the last time we had a storm like this!'

The disciples of Jesus were experienced fishermen but despite this, when confronted by this storm they were terrified.

 Charting the action

At the suggestion of Jesus, a flotilla of small boats set out in the evening to cross the Sea of Galilee. Tired from the exertion of preaching, he lay down in the stern with his head on a cushion and fell sound asleep.

The Lake of Galilee is notorious for sudden storms. The storm that hit that night was so ferocious the **terrified** disciples woke Jesus. He spoke to the wind and it died away. Then he rebuked his disciples for their lack of faith.

Noting the emotion

The occupants of the boat exhibited sheer **terror** when the 'furious squall' hit them (Matthew 4:37). Can't you see them clinging to the sides of the boat and screaming to Jesus for help? The three gospel accounts give interesting variations to their cries:

'Lord, save us! We're going to drown!' (Matthew 8:25)

'Teacher, don't you care if we drown?' (Mark 4:38)

'Master, Master, we're going to drown!' (Luke 8:24)

If these accounts were exactly the same it would suggest that one person wrote down this incident, and it was later copied.

Each man present probably shouted something slightly different. Imagine their **astonishment** when the wind died away in response to Jesus' command. Mark reports that they were **terrified**. Witnessing something supernatural troubled them. In **awe** they said to one another 'Who is this? Even the wind and the waves obey him!' (Mark 4:41)

 ## Extra comment

Many people allegorise this incident, likening it to our journey through life. Everything goes well until the storm of sin erupts. The disciples called out for help and we too can call on Jesus in prayer. In the same way that Jesus commanded the storm, he can control our evil desires if he is present in our lives.

This type of teaching can detract from the central lesson summed up in the disciples startled exclamation, 'What kind of man is this? Even the winds and the waves obey him!' (Matthew 8:27) There can be only one answer to that question, that Jesus is the Son of God.

For children

This incident is ready made for the quick sketch artist who can give a graphic description of the story and illustrate it at the same time.

One such illustration is still vivid in my mind. The speaker vigorously stirred water in a bucket then showed how the water kept swirling even after he stopped. He explained to the children that not only did the wind die away at Jesus' command but the swirling waves subsided as well. 'Even the wind *and* the waves obey him.'

THE DEMONIAC HEALED

 Focus Passage: Luke 8:26-39
Other references: Matthew 8:28-34
                      Mark 5:1-20

 Charting the action

After their distressing trip through the storm (vv. 22-25) Jesus and his disciples sailed to the region of the Gerasenes. When Jesus stepped ashore he was met by a demon possessed man living among the tombs (v. 27). This man shouted at Jesus and conversation between Jesus and the 'legion' of demons within him is reported. These pleaded with him not to order them to go into the abyss. Instead, they sought his permission to occupy a nearby herd of pigs. When this was granted, the demons entered the pigs. They became agitated and rushed over a nearby cliff and drowned (vv. 28-33).

The swineherds ran off to report what had happened and the people came out to see (vv. 34,35). At their request Jesus got into the boat to leave (v. 37). The man who had been healed pleaded to be allowed to accompany him, but Jesus refused his request and directed him to go home and report what God had done for him (vv. 38,39).

 Noting the emotion

The description of this tormented man fits a person in deep **distress**. 'Night and day among the tombs and in the hills he would cry out and cut himself with stones' (Mark 5:5).

His neighbours attempted to restrain him but the demons gave him superhuman strength and 'he tore the chains apart and broke the irons on his feet' (Mark 5:4).

As Jesus stepped from the boat 'he **ran** and **fell** on his knees in front of him. He **shouted** at the top of his voice' (Mark 5:6-7). The volume of the demons' challenge must have been at screaming pitch.

Once the demons had been exorcised there is a remarkable change, and the man is described as 'sitting there' (no longer agitated), 'dressed and in his right mind' (Mark 5:15).

'Those tending the pigs ran off and reported this in the town and the countryside' (Mark 5:14). They must have been very **excited** as their report stirred up a lot of interest. A crowd of sightseers soon gathered. The sight of the healed man filled them with fear and they 'pleaded' with Jesus to leave (Mark 5:17). 'This may have been a superstitious reaction to the supernatural power that had so evidently been in operation.' (Leon Morris, *Luke*, Tyndale New Testament Commentaries, IVP/Eerdmans, 1989)

The man must have been **upset** when he saw the **antagonism** of his neighbours and heard their demands for Jesus to leave, as he 'begged' Jesus to be allowed to accompany him. 'But Jesus sent him away saying "Return home and tell how much God has done for you."' (v. 39), a reversal of the usual instruction that Jesus gave to those who were healed.

The man proved to be a very effective witness, as he 'told all over the town how much Jesus had done for him.' (v. 39)

Extra comment

Some adults could be critical on hearing that the demons were sent into the pigs, because the man was cured at the expense of the owners of the animals, indeed at the expense of the animals. Children on the other hand, would have much more sympathy for the pigs.

Some suggest that as pigs were 'unclean' animals, the people should not have had them, but commentators seem to think that this indicates that the owners were Gentiles.

THE MAN AT THE POOL OF BETHESDA

 Focus Passage: John 5:1-14

This incident is significant because of the antagonism it aroused. It leads on to a very important discourse in which Jesus defends his claim to be the Son of God (vv. 17-30).

 Charting the action

The pool at Bethesda must have been a depressing place as a 'great number of disabled people' gathered at that place. These are described as blind, lame and paralysed.

The *Authorised Version* of the Bible informs us that they were 'waiting for the moving of the water'. This was attributed to the action of an angel who came down 'at a certain season and troubled the water'. The first person to step into the pool after this happened was healed of the ailment from which he or she suffered.

This explanation is omitted from more modern texts that use earlier manuscripts than those available to compilers of the *Authorised Version*. Obviously there must have been some reason why the needy congregated there and some expectation that the water could heal.

When Jesus passed by he challenged the man with the question, 'Do you want to get well?' (v. 6) He replied that he had no one to help him 'when the water is stirred' (v. 7) His reply is pathetic, revealing his misery. His had been a lengthy illness, thirty eight years in all, and the Lord may have sensed that after such a prolonged time the man had completely given up hope. Then Jesus said to him 'Get up! Pick up your mat and walk' (v. 8) Something in his tone stirred the man into action and he was immediately cured (v. 9).

 ## Noting the emotion

When a man is healed from an illness lasting thirty-eight years you would think everyone would be overjoyed. Sadly, this was not the case.

The healing occurred on a Sabbath. The man must have been **startled** when people he met accused him of breaking the Sabbath rules because he was carrying his mat (v. 10). He defended his action by explaining that the man who had healed him had told him to do it (11). He just couldn't win. His accusers ignore the miracle and focus on the Sabbath rule, trying to pinpoint who directed the man to disobey the religious law and carry his mat (v. 12). But when challenged to identify the person who had healed him the man was unable to do so. He 'had no idea who it was, for Jesus had slipped away into the crowd' (v. 13). The man must have been **bewildered** by all that was happening.

Later, after Jesus met him and instructed him to stop sinning, the man 'went away and told the Jews that it was Jesus who had made him well' (v. 15). The outcome of this was that persecution of Jesus was intensified because he 'was doing these things on the Sabbath' (v. 16). When challenged by the Jews, Jesus replied 'My Father is always at his work to this very day, and I, too, am working' (v. 17).

This aroused intense **hatred**. 'For this reason the Jews *tried all the harder to kill him*; not only was he breaking the

Sabbath, but he was even calling God his own Father, making himself equal with God' (v. 18).

 Extra comment

In the following discourse (vv. 36-47) the Lord lists five witnesses who testify to the validity of his claims – John the Baptist, the works he does, the Father, the Scriptures and Moses. He is aware, however, that his accusers will not accept their testimony. 'You refuse to come to me to have life' (v. 40).

FEEDING THE FIVE THOUSAND

    Focus Passage: *John 6:1-15*
    Other references: *Matthew 14:13-21*
                Mark 6:30-44
                Luke 9:10-17

Food looms large in our thinking. How often have you asked someone who has been away at a conference, a camp or on a trip, 'What was the food like?'

 Charting the action

John tells us that a 'great crowd' of people followed Jesus when he crossed over to the 'far shore of the Sea of Galilee' (John 4:1,2). This was an isolated area so the problem of how to provide food for these people soon became apparent. 'Where shall we buy bread for these people to eat?' (v. 5)

Andrew discovered a boy with five small barley loaves and two small fish and brought him to Jesus. Jesus directed his friends to organise the people into groups and to sit them down on the 'green grass' (Mark 6:39). After giving thanks he broke the bread and ordered his disciples to distribute it to the people.

Miraculously the food multiplied. There was sufficient to feed five thousand men plus women and children. At the conclusion of the meal the scraps filled twelve baskets.

 ## Noting the emotion

'Where shall we buy bread for these people to eat?' (v. 5)

Poor Philip, we are told that the purpose of Jesus' question was to test him (v. 6). He didn't pass the test. His **exasperation** is revealed in his reply 'Eight months' wages would not buy enough bread for each one to have a bite!' (v. 7)

We are not told the reactions of the disciples when they saw the tiny handful of food multiply but the reaction of the crowd is most dramatic. 'Surely this is the Prophet who is to come into the world' (v. 14). When they discussed this Jesus realised they would soon circulate the idea to make him their king. So Jesus sent his disciples away and 'went up a mountain, where he could be alone' (v. 15 CEV).

 ## Extra comment

Later in the chapter (6:25ff.) we have an extension of this event. Here Jesus focuses attention on what people need to learn from this miracle. He accuses the people who followed him round the Lake, that they pursued him for the wrong reason: 'I tell you for certain that you are not looking for me because you saw the miracles, but because you ate all the food you wanted' (v. 26 CEV).

He is hinting strongly that they have followed him in the hope of getting another free feed. He follows this up with the warning, 'Don't work for food that spoils. Work for food that gives eternal life. The Son of Man will give you this food, because God the Father has given him the right to do so' (v. 27 CEV).

Now study the discourse on the Bread of Life that follows. Note how the people are described as both 'grumbling' and 'arguing' (vv. 41,52 CEV). Jesus' message was not readily accepted and some, described as disciples, found it too hard and 'turned their backs on him and stopped following him' (v. 66 CEV). At this point Peter, as spokesman for the twelve in answer to Jesus' question as to whether they too would leave him, declared:

'Lord, there's no one else that we can go to! Your words give eternal life. We have faith in you, and we are sure that you are God's Holy One' (vv. 68-69 CEV).

 For children

Most people in children's ministry have used this story at some time. One reason for its popularity is that a little boy provided the loaves and fishes, so the story can be told from his point of view.

Today our children are bombarded with Lotto advertisements or the like on TV, where material prosperity is portrayed as the secret of happiness. So Jesus' message about not spending our energies for things that won't last is very relevant.

JESUS WALKS ON THE WATER

 Focus Passage: Matthew 14:22-33
Other references: Mark 6:45-52
John 6:16-24

There is probably no other incident in the record of the life of our Lord that is subject to as much ridicule as this event. To walk on water is a physical impossibility. It would appear that this spectacular display of power over nature happened when Jesus saw that the disciples were in difficulties, 'straining at the oars, because the wind was against them' (Mark 6:48), and this led to his rescue operation.

Charting the action

This event took place immediately after the miraculous meal that Jesus provided. As mentioned earlier by John, Jesus sent his disciples away by boat, then went off alone because the crowd was considering making him a king.

By the time Jesus caught up with them, the disciples had rowed a 'considerable distance' (Matthew 14:24) from the shore, 'four or five kilometres' (John 6:19 CEV), but it was tough going. Then they saw Jesus coming towards them, walking on the water. This **alarmed** them but Jesus reassured them and Peter asked if he could walk to Jesus. All went well until Peter, becoming aware of the elements, began to sink. Jesus caught him, then the two climbed into the boat and the wind died down (Matthew 14:25-32).

 ## Noting the emotion

'When the disciples saw him walking on the lake, they were terrified' (v. 26). 'It's a -, it's a -, g-g-ghost!' they shrieked. Immediately Jesus reassured them, 'I am Jesus! Don't be afraid!' (v. 27 CEV)

It is only Matthew's account that reports Peter saying to Jesus, 'Lord, if it's you tell me to come to you on the water' (v. 28). He seems to be seeking **reassurance**.

How **exhilarating** those first few steps must have been for Peter as he discovered he could walk on the waves. But then **fear** overwhelmed him and he began to sink. His 'Lord save me' must have been a **desperate** cry, and **relief** would have flooded his heart as Jesus' strong hand grasped his and lifted him up. Those who were in the boat were overwhelmed. They **worshipped** Jesus saying, 'Truly you are the Son of God' (v. 33)

 ## Extra comment

Mark concludes his account with a different emphasis, noting that when Jesus climbed into the boat, the disciples were 'completely amazed for they had not understood about the loaves; their hearts were hardened' (Mark 6:52).

 For children

A friend of mine, Robert Johnson, wrote an article recounting this incident from the viewpoint of a crab on the floor of the lake. He accompanied this with a series of clever illustrations depicting the soles of the feet of the people involved, as seen from below. Amazing what a little imagination can do!

HEALING THE CENTURION'S SERVANT

 Focus Passage: Luke 7:1-10
Other reference: Matthew 8:5-13

This incident features a remarkable man. Despite being a member of a conquering nation, he is described by the Jewish elders as one who 'loves our nation'. His admiration for the Jewish people was given practical expression for he provided funds to build a synagogue. A town the size of Capernaum would have a number of synagogues, but this one is described as 'our synagogue', indicating the affection these elders had for their building.

 Charting the action

A servant 'valued highly' by his employer was desperately ill and 'about to die'. Having heard of Jesus, this centurion persuaded some of the Jewish elders to approach Jesus on his behalf. Having been asked, Jesus started off towards the centurion's home. Then a further deputation of the centurion's friends met them with a request from the centurion that Jesus just 'say the word and my servant will be healed' (Luke 7:1,2,7).

Jesus expressed surprise, then turned and addressed the crowd around him drawing attention to the centurion's faith. The centurion's friends returned to his home and found the servant cured.

 ## Noting the emotion

The centurion was clearly **disturbed** at the prospect of losing his servant and resorted to desperate measures, asking the Jewish elders to represent him to Jesus. I can envisage him impressing on them how urgent it was.

This incident took place early in Jesus' ministry. The elders show no hesitation, hurrying to Jesus and '**pleading earnestly**' for his help in restoring the servant to health and strength. Their action demonstrates that they considered Jesus capable of performing this cure. Notice their words: 'This man deserves to have you do this' (v. 4).

Then the second group arrived with a new message saying it was unnecessary for Jesus to come, which Jesus found **astonishing**: 'In all of Israel I've never found anyone with this much faith!' (v. 9 CEV)

 ## Extra comment

Matthew's account adds a warning to the Jews that it was possible that God could reject them. Using the analogy of a heavenly feast, Jesus tells them that in God's sight, people of all races are equal. 'Many will come from the east and the west', indicates that guests will not only come from distant places but from differing cultural backgrounds as well. They would take their places at the feast along 'with Abraham, Isaac and Jacob in the kingdom of heaven' (Matthew 8:11).

We do not know how these Jewish elders reacted, but statements like these eventually led to the rejection of Jesus by senior Jews.

Is there a place card at that banquet with your name on it?

Cross check
See the note on 'faith' under the section about the woman who touched Jesus' coat, p. 76.

JESUS RAISES A WIDOW'S SON

 Focus Passage: Luke 7:11-17

 Charting the action

It must have been bedlam! Two large crowds arrived at the gateway of the little township of Nain. The one accompanying Jesus was trying to enter the gate just as a 'large' funeral procession was leaving it. What chaos as the two groups crossed paths.

Seeing the mother of the dead young man (v. 13), Jesus touched the coffin. Those carrying it 'stood still'. 'Young man, I say to you, get up!' (v. 14), said Jesus. 'The dead man sat up and began to talk, and Jesus gave him back to his mother' (v. 15).

 Noting the emotion

The local people following the coffin would have been **disconcerted** if not annoyed, when they suddenly found themselves surrounded by strangers who may not have appreciated the solemnity of the moment.

The dead person was 'the only son of his mother, and she was a widow' (v. 12). With no social security benefits in those days, the widow's plight would have been **desperate** for now there was no one to care for her. Is it any wonder that when Jesus saw her 'his heart went out to her'? 'Don't cry!' he said. Two words, but what **compassion, comfort** and **reassurance** they convey (v. 13).

Imagine the reaction of the people in both crowds when the young man 'sat up and began to talk' (v. 15). As he began to move some would be **terrified** but when Jesus 'gave him back to his mother', they realised he was really alive again, and the crowd was 'filled with **awe** and praised God' (v. 16).

Once again the chatter line came into operation as 'the news spread' (v. 17).

 ### Extra comment

Shortly afterwards a delegation from John the Baptist approached Jesus. They asked, 'Are you the one we should be looking for? Or must we wait for someone else?' (v. 19 CEV) Arriving in the thick of a campaign of healing of both a physical and spiritual nature, Jesus told them, 'Go and tell John what you have seen and heard. Blind people are now able to see, and the lame can walk. People who have leprosy are being healed, and the deaf can now hear. *The dead are raised to life*, and the poor are hearing the good news' (v. 22 CEV). The widow's son had become 'Exhibit A' in demonstrating this claim. (Compare this statement with Luke 4:18.)

 ### For children

It is not necessary to explain to children the taboos that normally prevent people from touching a coffin or a dead body, a difficult subject. It is sufficient to explain it was not normal for people to touch a coffin or dead body in those days, so when Jesus touched the coffin those who were carrying it stopped walking, perhaps out of astonishment. They would have been uncertain what to do next.

THE RAISING OF JAIRUS' DAUGHTER

Focus Passage: Mark 5:21-43
Other references: Luke 8:40-56
Matthew 9:18-26

Although this incident is intermingled with the healing of the woman who touched Jesus' clothes, it is helpful to consider the two events separately.

 Charting the action

Arriving after another lake crossing, Jesus was besieged by a large crowd (Mark 5:21). Among the crowd was one of the synagogue rulers, Jairus, who asked Jesus to help him because his daughter was dying (vv. 22,23). Jesus went with him and the crowd followed, making progress slow. The incident where the woman pressed through the crowd and touched Jesus' cloak then occurred and while Jesus was 'still speaking' to her, messengers came to inform Jairus that his daughter had died (v.35).

Jesus immediately reassured Jairus that all was not lost, and taking only three of his disciples, they continued on to Jairus' house (vv. 36,37).

On arrival, they found the place already surrounded by mourners. When Jesus told them the girl was not dead but only asleep their wailing turned to laughter (vv. 38-40). Ordering all the people out of the house except the parents and his disciples, Jesus went to where the girl was lying. Taking her hand he told her to get up. At that moment life was restored to her. Jesus told her parents to keep the matter quiet and to give her something to eat (vv. 40-43).

Noting the emotion

It is hard to grasp the full significance of the actions of Jairus – a man of his status falling at the feet of an itinerant preacher, pleading with him to come to his house to heal his daughter. Commentators suggest that he may have been part of the deputation of elders who previously approached Jesus on behalf of the Roman centurion. Now in desperate need himself, he came to Jesus, pleading for help.

Grief may have made his words almost incoherent, so when recounting the story, convey this sense to your audience. When they were interrupted by the woman on their way to his home, Jairus must first have been **irritated** and **perturbed** then **exasperated** as Jesus took time to speak to the woman.

And then when his servants arrived to tell him that his daughter was dead, Jairus must have been **overwhelmed** with despair. He would have turned dejectedly to Jesus, with tears in his eyes, a lump in his throat and a heavy heart. Then his hope would be rekindled by the words, 'Don't be afraid, just believe' (v. 36) Jairus had already shown faith by coming to Jesus, now he had to continue believing.

Arriving at his home they met with a commotion. People were already crying and wailing, well into their mourning routine.

'Why all this commotion and wailing?' Jesus asked. 'The child is not dead but asleep' (v. 39). Instantly their wailing turned to **laughter**. Imagine them saying, 'Ha! Ha! Listen to him! Asleep? She's dead. Ha! Ha!'

Jesus ordered nearly everyone out of the house and went in to where the girl was. He took her hand and said 'Little girl, I say to you, get up!'

Imagine the conflicting emotions of **astonishment** and **delight** that must have flitted across her parents' faces when she responded to his touch and his command. They were 'completely astonished', especially when she got up and 'walked around' (v. 42).

Extra comment

The New Testament, including Mark's account is written in Greek. It has always puzzled me as to why the Aramaic words, '*Talitha koum*' (which means 'little girl get up' in the vernacular language of Jesus' day) are included in this account. Cranfield and other Bible commentators suggest that these words were remembered and valued because they were the actual words used by Jesus on that memorable occasion. Commentators add much to our knowledge of the Bible.

 For children

This delightful story will employ almost all your story telling skills. You will plead with Jesus for help, jig from one foot to the other during the interruption, walk away dejectedly on hearing the grim news, and look up hopefully as Jesus encourages you to keep on believing. The wailing crowd and their ensuing laughter, the astonishment of the parents and the humorous touch where the parents are told to give her something to eat, all of these emotions are waiting for you to bring them to life.

THE WOMAN WHO TOUCHED HIS COAT

    Focus Passages: Mark 5:25-34
Luke 8:43-48

Both Mark and Luke report this happening in detail. Read them together as each contributes something extra to the other version.

On his way to Jairus' house Jesus was interrupted by a pathetic figure, a woman with a chronic medical complaint that had persisted for twelve years. Remedies prescribed by 'many doctors' had exhausted all her financial resources and despite this, 'instead of getting better she grew worse' (Mark 5:26).

 ### Charting the action

The crowd accompanying Jairus and Jesus that day was so big that Jesus was almost 'crushed' by the pressure of the people packed around him. Recognising Jesus and believing he could heal her, the woman wormed her way through the crowd until she was able to reach out her hand and touch him. 'Immediately her bleeding stopped' (Luke 8:44).

Jesus stopped and enquired who had touched him. Realising that Jesus knew what she had done, the woman came forward and 'told why she had touched him and how she had been instantly healed.' Jesus reassured her that she was healed and told her to 'Go in peace' (Luke 8:47,48).

 ### Noting the emotion

Picture the woman's face, probably lined and tense, revealing her battle with the debilitating illness she had **endured** for twelve years. Seeing Jesus, she grasps her one opportunity for healing. Imagine her **exhilaration** when moments after touching his coat she realises she is cured. But then, Jesus stops and demands to know who has touched him. Her moment of **joy** is shattered.

To the dense crowd packed around Jesus, his question was ridiculous. '"You see the people crowding against you," his disciples answered "and yet you can ask, who touched me?"' (Mark 5:31) Luke reports that 'all denied it,' with Peter saying, 'Master, the people are crowding and pressing against you' (Luke 8:45).

'Someone touched me; I know that power has gone out from me.' Hearing this, the woman realised that her action could not go 'unnoticed' as she had hoped. Trembling with **fear** she pushed her way through the crowd. Falling at Jesus' feet, she told him what she had done. 'Daughter, your faith has healed you. Go in peace, and be freed from your suffering' (Mark 5:34).

Extra comment

In society at that time, a woman with a chronic bleeding problem was treated in much the same way as a leper. Regulations concerning this are found in Leviticus 15:25ff. To be touched by such a person resulted in ceremonial uncleanness, so in practice, the person with the problem was excluded from taking part in normal society.

Compassion for sufferers like this woman led Jesus to ignore these restraints. He had already touched a leper and a coffin, and now this woman had touched him. Matthew 8:17 points out that Jesus fulfilled what was spoken through the prophet Isaiah: 'He took up our infirmities and carried our diseases' (Isaiah 53:4).

Jesus addresses this woman as 'daughter', the only time he uses this word in the gospel record. It conveys warmth, comfort and intimacy.

For children

The nature of this woman's complaint presents a bit of a difficulty for small children, so it is best to gloss over her problem and merely report that she had been sick for twelve years.

The woman is told that her faith had healed her. Faith has three ingredients:

- **Knowledge:** 'when she heard about Jesus',
- **Belief:** She thought, 'If I just touch his clothes I will be healed' and,
- **Trust:** She reached out her hand and 'touched his cloak.'

These three steps of faith can be linked to any number of incidents where faith is seen in operation. They are a helpful way for children to remember what is meant by faith.

THE MAN WITH THE CRIPPLED HAND

Focus Passage: *Mark 3:1-6*
Other references: *Matthew 12:9-14*
                    Luke 6:6-11

'Stand up in front of everyone' (Mark 3:1). None of us enjoys being made a spectacle, especially those of us with some disability. Jesus could have healed this man unobtrusively but preferred to confront those present who were 'looking for a reason to accuse' him (v. 2).

 ## Charting the action

When Jesus entered the synagogue he noticed a man with a crippled hand. It was the Sabbath and Jesus was aware that some people present were watching to see if he would break the Sabbath rules. Jesus challenged them to determine whether or not it was right to do good on the Sabbath.

Receiving no response he ordered the man to stretch out his hand. Immediately his hand was 'completely restored' (v. 5).

 ## Noting the emotion

The Pharisees and teachers of the law were poised like a flock of vultures **watching him closely** to see if he would heal on the Sabbath (Luke 6:7). Under such close scrutiny it is unlikely that he could have helped the man unobtrusively. Jesus 'knew what they were thinking' (Luke 6:8) and ordered the man to stand up. Jesus addressed those whom he knew were waiting to criticise him – 'On the Sabbath should we do good deeds or evil deeds? Should we save someone's life or destroy it?' (Mark 3:4 CEV) He was attempting to stir their consciences. He wanted them to see that failure to do good was to do evil. 'But no one said a word' (v. 4 CEV).

These hard-hearted men were only interested in finding some reason to accuse Jesus. They had no concern for the plight of the invalid.

Meanwhile the man was standing there. We are not told what his reactions were but he must have been feeling **awkward**. In Matthew's account, Jesus continues to press his point by referring to the Pharisees' practice of setting the Sabbath rule aside in an emergency. 'If any of you has a sheep and it falls into a pit on the Sabbath, will you not take hold of it and lift it out? How much more valuable is a man than a sheep? Therefore it is lawful to do good on the Sabbath' (Matthew 12: 11-12). Although this argument could not be disputed, it failed to move the Pharisees. They maintained their stony silence.

'Jesus was **angry** as he looked around at the people. Yet he **felt sorry** for them because they were so stubborn.' Turning to the man he said, 'Stretch out your hand' (Mark 3:5 CEV). The command of the Lord supplied the power to respond.

The Pharisees could not claim he had broken any ruling. He had not touched the man nor had he encouraged him to exercise his recovered power.

They were **furious**. Mark reports that they 'started making plans with Herod's followers to kill Jesus' (Mark 3:6 CEV).

To reach this point, clearly their opposition was hardening.

 Extra comment

Three major groups were part of the political scene at that time: The Sadducees who mainly represented the priestly caste, the Pharisees who included the teachers of the law, and the Herodians who supported King Herod. As Jesus was Herod's subject, it was important for them to turn Herod against him.

JESUS HEALS THE SYRO-PHOENICIAN'S DAUGHTER

Focus Passage: *Matthew 15:21-28*
Other references: Mark 7:24-30

This incident took place on one of Jesus' rare excursions outside of Jewish territory. Mark reports that he did not want anyone to know he was there but his presence could not be kept secret.

 ## Charting the action

Just who spotted Jesus and reported his presence is not known but the word spread like wildfire. A Greek woman born in Syrian Phoenicia heard the news and hurried to him to appeal for her daughter's healing. Her little daughter was demon possessed.

Initially her plea was ignored but due to her tenacity she was finally rewarded. 'At that moment her daughter was healed' (15:28 CEV).

 ## Noting the emotion

It is never easy to be ignored. This desperate woman must have been **frustrated** when Jesus 'did not answer a word' (v. 23) in response to her appeal. Perhaps her appeal to him as the Son of David was inappropriate, coming from a foreigner's lips.

The woman's cry continued incessantly and she became a nuisance. The disciples were **irritated** (v. 23), 'for she keeps crying out after us'. Implied in their suggestion to send her away, is for Jesus to do what she wants so they can be rid of her.

But Jesus was in no mood to curtail his ministry to Israel for any gentile. The woman persists in her appeal, kneeling before him, an indication of her **anguish**.

Her appeal is simple and direct, 'Lord help me!' (v. 25)

'She concludes that the door is shut against her, not for the purpose of excluding her altogether, but that, by a more strenuous effort of faith, she may force her way, as it were, through the chinks.' (Calvin)

Jesus seems to think the door is shut for he says, 'It isn't right to take food away from children and feed it to dogs' (v. 26 CEV).

The woman even accepts the tag with which Jesus labelled her. The gist of her reply is:

'What you say is true Lord. Let me share the position not of the children but of the dogs. Even the dogs aren't prevented from licking up the crumbs that fall from their owner's table.' This response delights Jesus: 'Woman, you have great faith. Your request is granted.' (Matthew 15:28)

Imagine her **delight** when 'she went home and found her child lying on the bed, and the demon gone' (Mark 7:30).

 ## Extra comment

From a Jewish perspective, foreigners were 'dogs'. As the word in the Greek means 'little dogs', Jesus is probably referring to the puppies that had access to the households in contrast to the street dogs.

 ## For children

It may be unwise to attempt to use this story for children, as the issues involved in understanding this situation are complex.

JESUS HEALS THE MAN BORN BLIND

 Focus Passage: John 9:1-41

Because I did not understand why the Lord made clay from his spittle to cure this blind man, I avoided this story for years. I found the key to it in the writings of Professor Blaiklock. He pointed out that in those days there was a belief that the spittle of a good man had healing qualities. This man did not know who Jesus was. Blaiklock suggests that Jesus' purpose in mixing the clay with his spittle was to 'ignite the spark of faith'.

Believing Jesus to be a good man gave the blind man reason to hope for a cure.

 ## Charting the action

After smearing the clay on the man's eyes Jesus ordered him to wash it off in the pool of Siloam. When he returned able to see (v. 7), his neighbours gathered round wondering what had happened. They took the man to be examined by the Pharisees (v. 13).

They in turn sent for his parents to ascertain whether he really had been blind and what had happened to him (vv. 18,19). After an extended conversation, the Pharisees became so enraged that they threw the man out of the synagogue (v. 34). Jesus then heard what had happened to him and went looking for him. He introduced himself to him, resulting in the man's adulation (vv. 35-38).

 ## Noting the emotion

If you have ever tried to open a bank account you will know something of this man's **frustration**. Bank staff require a multiplicity of identifications from you to prove your identity.

Imagine being subjected to the following conversation about you as you stand by, a frustrated onlooker:

'Isn't this the same man who used to sit and beg?'

'Yes, I'm sure it's the same man!'

'No, he only looks like him.'

Can't you see his mouth gaping open in **astonishment** as he protests 'I am the man?' (v. 9)

'How come you can see?'

The healed man patiently describes what happened to him explaining how Jesus had put mud on his eyes and ordered him to wash. 'I went and washed, and then I could see' (v. 11).

The miraculous healing happened on a Sabbath, and as on many other occasions, this issue complicated the discussion.

Questioned by the Pharisees the man repeated the sequence of events that led to the restoration of his sight. His recital met with another conversation, one where he was a spectator only.

Finally they turned back to him and asked, 'What have you to say about him?' His reply is little more than a guess: 'He is a prophet' (v. 17).

Some were still doubtful about his identity and question the man's parents who faced a barrage of **aggressive** questions:

'Is this your son?'

'Is this the one who was born blind?'

'How is it that he can now see?'

The parents answer very **cautiously**. 'We are certain that he is our son, and we know that he was born blind. But we don't know how he got his sight or who gave it to him. Ask him! He is old enough to speak for himself' (v. 20 CEV).

John explains that the reason for their caution was the threat of excommunication from the synagogue.

They called the man in again and, in what must have been an aggressive tone, demanded he 'swear by God to tell the truth! We know that Jesus man is a sinner' (v. 24 CEV). Obviously they are making this judgment because Jesus had broken the Sabbath rules.

The man is very **patient**. 'Whether he is a sinner or not, I don't know. One thing I do know. I was blind but now I see!' (v. 25) When they asked him to repeat what had happened to him his patience wore thin. 'I have told you already and you did not listen. Why do you want to hear it again? *Do you want to become his disciples too?*'

If this question was intended to provoke them it had the desired effect. The Pharisees became **agitated** and they 'hurled insults at him' (v. 28). There is a mixture of **disdain** and **pomposity** in their reply. 'You are this fellow's disciple! We are disciples of Moses!' That was a bit rough considering the man didn't even know Jesus. Can't you see the superior looks on their faces?

'We know that God spoke to Moses, but as for this fellow, we don't even know where he comes from' (v. 29). Could this be a reference to Jesus' doubtful parentage?

Notice too, how they avoid speaking about Jesus by name and **scornfully** refer to him as 'this fellow'.

Don't you love his reply?

'Now that is remarkable! You don't know where he comes from, yet he opened my eyes. We know that God does not listen to sinners. He listens to the godly man who does his will. Nobody has ever heard of opening the eyes of a man born blind. If this man were not from God, he could do nothing' (vv. 30-32).

The man had come a long way in his understanding in a short time, hadn't he?

'To this they replied, "You were steeped in sin at birth; how dare you lecture us!" and they threw him out' (v. 34). This final phrase seems to indicate a screaming mob physically hustling him out the door.

The tempo of the record changes at this point. It becomes quieter and more dignified as Jesus seeks out the man, asking him whether he believed in the Son of Man. His reply reveals that he is still ignorant of who Jesus is, the Son of Man. '"You've already seen him" Jesus answered, "and right now he is talking with you"' (v. 37 CEV). Then the man said, 'Lord I believe', and worshipped him (v. 38).

 Extra comment

The development of the man's faith provides a good pattern for a sermon.

In the first instance the man is very vague about Jesus. He describes him as 'the man they call Jesus'. When challenged to offer an opinion about Jesus he makes some progress as he declares 'he is a prophet'. His experience of having his sight restored is so real that he makes further progress saying, 'if this man were not from God he could do nothing'. Finally Jesus reveals to him who he is and the man declares his faith with, 'Lord I believe'. He then worships Jesus.

When we first meet the man in his blind state the disciples asked the question 'Who sinned, this man or his parents, that he was born blind?' This records the popular concept that physical disability was due to sin. Jesus instantly corrects this and explains that the purpose of the man's blindness is so that 'the work of God might be displayed in his life' (v. 3). Later when the Pharisees abused the man by saying 'You were steeped in sin at birth' (v. 34), they were affirming the belief that his blindness must have been due to sin.

AT THE HOME OF MARY AND MARTHA

 Focus Passage: Luke 10:38-42

 Charting the action

'As Jesus and his disciples were on their way' (v. 38).

This phrase is repeated numerous times in the New Testament. Each time there is no indication of where they were coming from nor their destination.

'Martha opened her home to him' (v. 38), seems to indicate that this was his first contact with this family who will feature from time to time in the record.

Martha is soon busily employed preparing a meal and protests because her sister, Mary, does not help her (v. 40).

 ## Noting the emotion

What did Martha know of Jesus to invite him into her home? Perhaps she knew something of him and was excited when he accepted the invitation.

She bustled about to provide the very best for her honoured guests. By contrast Mary, her sister, preferred to sit and listen to Jesus. This **irritated** Martha and her **frustration** became so intense that she complained to Jesus. 'Lord, doesn't it bother you that my sister has left me to do all the work by myself? Tell her to come and help me!' (v. 40 CEV)

Jesus recognises her frustration and seeks to comfort her. 'You are **worried** and **upset** about so many things, but only one thing is necessary' (vv. 41-42 CEV). He may have meant by this that an elaborate meal wasn't necessary, something simple was sufficient.

Despite his evident **patience** with Martha he would not accede to her request. He recognises that Mary's desire is to learn from him and he quietly but firmly states that 'Mary has chosen what is best, and it won't be taken away from her' (v. 42 CEV).

 ## Extra comment

Later glimpses of the characters of two women are consistent with what we witness here. When their brother, Lazarus, died they sent for Jesus. After considerable delay, Jesus arrived at their home and Martha, the more aggressive one, hurried out to meet him. Mary 'stayed in the house' (John 11:20).

We see another glimpse when Jesus visited Bethany again and was entertained with a meal. 'Martha served', while Mary expressed her devotion by pouring expensive perfume on Jesus' feet, an action Jesus described as pointing to his burial (John 12:2,3).

THE WIDOW'S OFFERING

 Focus Passage: *Luke 21:1-4*

Four short verses, but what a powerful story.

 ## Charting the action

We need to turn back to the previous chapter to set the scene of this action.

'One day Jesus was teaching in the temple and telling the good news' (Luke 20:1 CEV).

It was while he was here that a delegation approached him, attempting to trap him with a question about tax. This was followed by questions from the Sadducees on the issue of the resurrection. Following these challenges Jesus warned his disciples to be on guard against the teachers of the law. He had some harsh words of condemnation against these, including the claim that they 'cheat widows out of their houses' Luke 20:47).

It is then that he observed a widow placing her offering in the offertory box and called the attention of his disciples to her action.

 ## Noting the emotion

The widow's action can be described as absolute **devotion**.

Jesus had noticed a procession of 'rich' people 'tossing their gifts into the 'treasury', a row of thirteen trumpet shaped collection boxes, as he sat teaching in the Temple. There was nothing unobtrusive about their actions.

Possibly they wanted to be noticed. Many may have given generously but the Lord's attention was attracted to a 'poor widow', whose gift was 'two very small copper coins' (v. 2).

He **excitedly** called the attention of his disciples to her **sacrificial** action. He explained to them that hers was a true love gift. 'I tell you that this poor woman has put in more than all the others. Everyone else gave what they didn't need. But she is very poor and gave everything she had' (vv. 3-4 CEV).

 Extra comment

This story links with 2 Corinthians 9 where Paul speaks about the right way to give. Despite her abject poverty the widow gave out of a **thankful** heart.

THE RAISING OF LAZARUS

 Focus Passage: John 11:1-44

Do you know the saying 'It's the last straw that breaks the camel's back'?

Commentators suggest that the raising of Lazarus was the last straw for the chief priests, for from that day on, they plotted to take Jesus' life (11:53).

 Charting the action

The action begins in the previous chapter, with the Jews threatening to stone Jesus because he claimed 'to be God' (10:33).

As the discussion progressed they 'tried to seize him, but he escaped their grasp' (10:39).

Antagonism intensified and Jesus 'went back across the Jordan to the place where John had been baptising in the early days' (10:40).

This place seems to have been a sanctuary and when messengers arrived to inform him that Lazarus was ill, he appeared to ignore them and made no response for two days (11:3,6).

When he told his disciples of his intention to return to Bethany they reminded him of his previous troubles and the threat of stoning (vv. 7,8). They may have discussed amongst themselves whether this was the reason he did not respond immediately to the appeal for help from Martha and Mary.

It must have been some distance to travel for by the time they arrived in Bethany Lazarus had been dead for four days (v. 17).

Martha was the first person to greet him. Mary came a little time later when Jesus sent for her (v. 20). Jesus then requested to be taken to Lazarus' grave, where despite protest from Martha, the stone covering the cave where he was buried was moved at Jesus' request (vv. 34, 38,39). After praying briefly Jesus commanded the dead man to come out of his grave. Lazarus stumbled out, still wrapped in grave clothes. Jesus ordered them to release him (vv. 41-44).

Some who witnessed the event informed the Pharisees. They called an emergency meeting of the Sanhedrin (v. 47), their Council, to discuss the matter. Knowing that they were plotting against him, Jesus went down to a village called Ephraim, 'near the desert' (v. 54).

The Feast of the Passover was drawing close when Jesus left his desert retreat and returned to Bethany. His friends entertained him there, and during the meal, Mary poured expensive perfume on Jesus' feet and wiped them with her hair. Jesus said that this action was preparation for his burial (12:1-3). Crowds gathered to see both him and Lazarus (12:9).

In their plans to kill Jesus, the chief priests included Lazarus. They wanted Lazarus back in his grave because 'He was the reason many of the Jewish people were turning from them and putting their faith in Jesus' (12:11 CEV).

Noting the emotion

You would have thought that the message the sisters, Mary and Martha sent to Jesus, which contained a strong appeal, would bring instant response: 'Lord the one you love is sick' (v. 3). What Jesus said when he received the news about Lazarus **puzzled** the disciples: 'This sickness will not end in death. No, it is for God's glory so that God's son may be glorified through it' (11:4).

Jesus frequently ordered people to keep the news of his healing activity to themselves. Now he intended to display his power so that he would be recognised as 'the resurrection and the life'.

His disciples were **startled** when he declared his intention to return to Bethany and gave expression to their **alarm** reminding him of the danger of stoning (vv. 7,8). Jesus explained that their concern was unnecessary; he was **confident** that no harm could come to him. Now he could travel safely, as a man walking in sunlight is untroubled by darkness (vv. 9,10). He knew that 'his hour' was approaching but it had not as yet arrived. Later, when arrested in the Garden of Gethsemane, Jesus said: 'This is your hour – when darkness reigns' (Luke 22:53).

Jesus explained to his disciples that he was returning to Bethany to wake Lazarus up from sleep. Their reaction was to assume that if Lazarus was asleep, this was a good indication that he was on the mend. But in case there was any doubt in their minds of the real situation, Jesus told them plainly 'Lazarus is dead' (v. 14).

Thomas reacted pessimistically to Jesus' intention to return to Bethany. 'Let us also go, that we may die with him' (v. 16).

On hearing of Jesus' arrival, Martha bustled out to meet him. She appears to have given Jesus a piece of her mind. 'Lord', she said, 'if you had been here, my brother would not have died' (vv. 20,21). What tone of voice did she use? My feeling is that she was inferring 'Why didn't you come when we sent for you?' Then, perhaps sensing she has been too blunt, she appears to soften her approach with the words, 'I know that even now God will give you whatever you ask' (v. 22).

In the conversation that followed, Martha makes a clear declaration of faith. 'I believe you are the Christ, the Son of God' (v. 27).

Returning to the house she tells Mary that 'The Teacher is here and is asking for you' (v. 28). Mary is **distressed** by the loss of her brother but responds immediately to the summons.

Her greeting, although identical to Martha's, suggests her voice had a different tone. Perhaps she inferred, 'if only you had come when we sent for you.' In her distress Mary fell at Jesus' feet and weeping. Others gathered there were also **weeping**. Seeing their anguish Jesus was '**deeply moved** in spirit and **troubled**', to the point where he too openly wept (vv. 33,35). Some of those with Mary noted how upset Jesus was, 'See how he loved him!' (v. 36) Others were more critical: if Jesus could restore sight miraculously then surely he could have cured Lazarus (v. 37).

When they arrived at the grave, Jesus ordered them to remove the stone. Martha's reaction is to the point. The Authorised Version of the Bible expresses it this way: 'Lord, by this time he stinketh for he has been dead for four days' (v. 39; 'stinketh' seems a stronger description than 'bad odour' NIV or 'bad smell' CEV).

After **patiently** reassuring her, Jesus prayed. Then in 'a loud voice', he called, 'Lazarus, come out!' (v. 43)

Picture the **alarm** on the faces of the gathered crowd. They would have shrunk back in horror as the mummified figure of Lazarus stumbled out of the tomb. Many who witnessed this spectacular event became believers (v. 45).

 ### Extra comment

Refer to a good commentary to help sort out the complexity of the discussion between Martha and Jesus. When Jesus seeks to comfort her with the assurance that her brother will rise again, Martha thinks he is speaking of 'the resurrection at the last day' (v. 24). One can almost hear her saying 'so what', as she shows little enthusiasm for what Jesus has said. When Jesus tells her that he is 'the resurrection and the life', he is urging her to trust him.

'To believe in Him is not only to be assured about the resurrection at the last day, but to experience here and now something of that eternal life to which resurrection is the prelude. Such a believer, though he must pass through physical death, as Lazarus has done, will go on living; and no-one who has faith in Jesus can ever perish.' (R.V.G. Tasker, *John*, Tyndale New Testament Commentaries, IVP/Eerdmans, 1989)

That Martha did not understand what this implied is evident by her reaction when Jesus ordered the stone be moved.

 For children

Many of us will have used the series of the 'I am' sayings of Jesus at talks given at house parties or camps. However, these concepts are not easy for children to grasp. Jesus' claim that he is the resurrection and the life is a complex claim. I find it difficult to explain the conversation Jesus had with Martha. We can say that if we have put our trust in him we look forward to being with Jesus in heaven after we die.

HEALING BLIND BARTIMAEUS

 Focus Passage: *Mark 10:46-52*
Other references: Matthew 20:29-34
                          Luke 18:35-43

 Charting the action

Jesus and his disciples visited the city of Jericho where a large crowd welcomed him enthusiastically. Bartimaeus, a blind beggar, asked the reason for the excitement and when he heard that Jesus was passing by, called to him for help.

Bartimaeus, despite his blindness, must have been tuned into the gossip of the streets as his shouting indicated that he knew something about Jesus. This contrasts with the blind man of John 9 who knew nothing about Jesus. Bartimaeus kept shouting despite attempts on the part of some of the crowd to silence him.

Jesus stopped and ordered them to bring the blind man to him. The man jumped up eagerly and threw his coat aside (v.50). This action is significant as a blind person cannot discard his possessions and expect to find them again. His action is a strong pointer to his belief that Jesus would be able to restore his sight.

When his sight was restored 'he went down the road with Jesus' (v. 52 CEV).

 ## Noting the emotion

When Jesus passed through the Jericho gateway, Bartimaeus was not going to miss his once in a lifetime opportunity. 'Jesus', he shouted 'Son of David, have pity on me!' (v. 47 CEV) He must have been very **agitated**. His shouting caused such a disturbance that many in the crowd tried to shut him up. Their **antagonism** must have been **distressing** but it only fired his determination and he 'shouted all the more' (v. 48).

When Jesus stopped and ordered them to call him their attitude changed and they became quite **helpful**. 'Cheer up!' they said. 'On your feet! He's calling you!' Bartimaeus' heart must have missed a beat when he heard this. 'He jumped up', an action that indicated his **eagerness**, and discarding his coat he 'ran to Jesus' (v. 50 CEV), a further indication of his **excitement**.

Jesus asked him, 'What do you want me to do for you?'

'Rabbi, I want to see' (v. 51).

'Receive your sight,' said Jesus. 'Your faith has healed you' (Luke 18:42).

It was an electrifying moment for Bartimaeus when his vision cleared.

When telling the story, I describe him laughing and skipping and shouting praises to God as he followed Jesus down the road.

The crowd that had seen what happened 'praising God' too (Luke 18:43). It was a **joyous** time.

 ### Extra comment

There are variations between the three accounts of this event. Matthew says there were two blind men, Mark's is the only one to supply the name, Bartimaeus. For Matthew and Mark the events occurred as Jesus was leaving Jericho, while Luke has Jesus approaching Jericho.

Of these conflicting reports, the Tyndale commentary says: 'with our present information it may be impossible to give a satisfactory explanation of these differences.'

 ### For children

See the sample outline on this story in the introductory section, entitled 'Planning the Flow', p. 8.

ZACCHAEUS THE TAX COLLECTOR

 Focus Passage: Luke 19:1-10

 ### Charting the action

When Zacchaeus, the chief tax collector in Jericho heard that Jesus was expected to visit their city, he was curious and joined the crowd. Being a short man, he was unable to see, so he climbed a tree to get a clearer view (vv. 3,4).

When Jesus reached this spot he stopped, called Zacchaeus down from his branch, then said that he intended to dine with Zacchaeus. The onlookers were critical, for Zacchaeus was not regarded well by the citizens of Jericho (vv. 5,7).

Resulting from his meeting with Jesus, Zacchaeus demonstrated true repentance, offering to make restitution to any he had cheated (v. 8).

 ## Noting the emotion

If this were Jesus' first and only visit to Jericho, this would account for the excitement of the crowds gathered to welcome him. **Curiosity** was Zacchaeus' motivation, but he was **frustrated** by the density of the crowd and by his shortness of height.

Anyone who has been in a crowd and has been unable to see what is going on will know something of his frustration. Zacchaeus was a **determined** person and **undaunted** by this difficulty. He quickly saw that a view from a tree would solve his problem.

Was his presence unobtrusive or did people notice him there? If they did, you could imagine them greeting with hilarity the sight of the chief tax collector climbing a tree.

'Hey, Zacchaeus! What are you doing up there? Are you trying to collect taxes from the birds?'

How do you think Zacchaeus felt when Jesus stopped right under his tree? And what would he have thought when Jesus called him by name?

We know from the record that his response to Jesus' call was instantaneous, and his welcome enthusiastic. 'He came down at once and **welcomed him gladly**' (v. 6). The bystanders were not as enthusiastic for they began to 'mutter'. 'He has gone to be the guest of a sinner' (v. 7). Later, Zacchaeus' announcement that he would distribute half of his goods to the poor and make restitution four times over to anyone he had cheated, must have **astonished** them (v. 8).

How do you think Zacchaeus felt when he heard Jesus say, 'Salvation has come to this man's house'? (v. 8) In our eagerness to explain the meaning of Jesus' words, we may miss describing the sense of **exhilaration** these words would bring to Zacchaeus.

 Extra comment

'He has gone to be the guest of a "sinner."¹' It is clear from this complaint that Zacchaeus was not highly regarded by his fellow citizens. Probably all tax collectors were considered sinners. The job carried a stigma because there was always the suspicion that the tax collector was cheating, and this gave the crowd cause to label him a 'sinner'. That he had indeed cheated the community seems evident from his offer to repay anyone he may have cheated, four times over. We need to remember too that sin is not only doing wrong but also not doing right (see James 4:17).

What had Zacchaeus failed to do? The declaration of his intentions gives a clue to the answer. 'Look, Lord! Here and now I give half of my possessions to the poor' (v. 8). Until Zacchaeus met Jesus, it is unlikely that he gave so much as a cent away. He was a self-centred man. Now his first action is to think of others and their welfare. Jesus responded with, 'Today, salvation has come to this house, because this man, too, is a son of Abraham' (v. 9).

'Salvation.' Who was Zacchaeus saved from? Himself! Jesus had liberated him from his self-centredness. 'To this house' (v. 9). This is an interesting phrase. We don't know whether Zacchaeus had a family but if he did then all would benefit from his transformation. A 'son of Abraham' (v. 9); Jesus indicated that Zacchaeus was now a person of worth. Abraham was a man of faith; all those who have faith can be described as his sons (see Galations 3:7).

For children

This is a favourite story of storytellers, and most children exposed to Christian instruction are familiar with it. So an alternative approach could be to focus on Jesus' closing statement, 'The Son of Man came to look for and to save people who are lost' (v. 10).

In your introduction you could centre on the idea of being lost, probably using a story about some child who was lost. Then you could lead on to describe Zacchaeus as a man who had everything – position, power and possessions – yet is described as lost by Jesus.

Zacchaeus was an outcast, despised by the people of his town. Until he met Jesus he was going his own way, thinking only of himself. Even Zacchaeus was valuable to God. Jesus' purpose is to look for and save people who are lost.

PAYING TAXES TO CAESAR

 Focus Passage: Matthew 22:15-22
Other references: Mark 12:13-17
Luke 20:20-26

In Mark and Luke, this incident is recorded immediately after Jesus spoke about the unfaithful tenants in the vineyard. So the teachers of the law and the chief priests knew that he had spoken this parable against them and 'looked for a way to arrest him immediately' (Luke 20:19). They needed an excuse to be able to accuse him, so they 'laid plans to trap him in his words' (Matthew 22:15).

 Charting the action

To execute their plan against Jesus, the Pharisees formed an alliance with the Herodians. Discussions had already begun with them (see p. 58). The Pharisees hated paying taxes to the Romans, although the Herodians were happy with the system. So the question relating to the tax could be seen as asking Jesus to adjudicate in a difference of opinion.

To make the trap less obvious, the leading Pharisees did not go themselves but sent some of 'their disciples' (v. 15) to represent them. Despite their well orchestrated planning, Jesus saw through their subterfuge immediately (v. 18).

 ## Noting the emotion

'We know you are a man of integrity and that you teach the way of God in accordance with the truth' (v. 16). The opening remarks of the delegation are pleasant and flattering. Yet behind the surface politeness, it is obvious they have not accepted the teaching of Jesus and are not prepared to follow it. They continue their flattery by appearing to appreciate his forthrightness: 'You are not swayed by men, because you pay no attention to who they are' (v. 16). They appear to value his insights for they ask, 'Tell us then, what is your opinion? Is it right to pay taxes to Caesar or not?' (v. 17).

But if Jesus agreed, his answer would put him offside with the people. If he answered in the negative, he would fall foul of the Romans and they would have grounds to report him. So Jesus could not win either way.

But Jesus 'saw through their duplicity' (Luke 20:23) and his answer is brutally blunt. 'You hypocrites, why are you trying to trap me? Show me the coin used for paying the tax' (Matthew 22:19). When the coin was brought to him (they may have had to send out to the moneychangers in the courtyard to obtain the 'denarius' he asked for) he challenged them with the question, 'Whose portrait is this? And whose inscription?' (v. 20). One side of the coin would have had the features of the Emperor Tiberius and on the other, the title 'Pontifex Maximus.'

'Caesar's!' was their reply (v. 21).

The Jews believed that to accept the coinage of any king was to acknowledge his supremacy. By using the denarius as an everyday coin, they were already openly declaring

Caesar's sovereignty and thus by their action had already answered their question as to whether they should pay the poll tax. 'Give to Caesar what is Caesar's!' If it is his they should give it back to him. Jesus then went on to say, give 'to God what is God's' (v. 21). Because you are his, you should let him have full control of your lives.

What he said **amazed** them and 'they were silent' (v. 34). Despite their failure to trap him with the tax question their deceit was to resurface at Jesus' trial when they would say to Pilate, 'He opposes payment of taxes to Caesar' (Luke 23:2).

 Extra comment

The coin was marked with Caesar's image. We are made in the 'image of God' (Genesis 1:27). This means there are certain things about us that are different from all other animals. Our personalities, our individuality and our ability to recognise right from wrong, all are indications that we carry the image of God.

THE BLIND MAN AT BETHSAIDA

 Focus Passage: Mark 8:22-26

In the Introduction to this book, I referred to some schoolgirls who expressed doubt about the historical existence of Jesus. Later in the week I addressed the assembly at that school on the subject, 'Did Jesus ever exist?'

I approached the subject from the position that the incidents reported in the gospels are either historical events or a collection of myths. I pointed out that if they were only myths, how strange some of the stories appear. As an example, I selected this report of the healing of the blind man at Bethsaida. It is quite likely that someone might invent a mythical character with the power to perform miraculous acts of healing. However, it seems inconceivable that any writer would dream up a story like this one, where the miracle healer had to make a second attempt as the first effort was only partly effective. This story is unique in the New Testament, though the cure of the deaf mute in Mark 7:31-37 also involved considerable effort.

 ## Charting the action

Once again we see friends in action bringing a blind man to Jesus. Jesus led the blind man outside the village, presumably to obtain privacy. He used spit on the man's eyes then touched him, asking the man whether he could 'see anything'. The man's reply is vague. 'I see people; they look like trees walking around.'

Jesus then placed his hands on the man's eyes a second time and he 'saw everything clearly'.

Jesus instructed him to go home without going back to the village.

 ## Noting the emotion

The only direct reference to emotion found in the passage is that of the people who brought the blind man to Jesus. They **begged** Jesus to touch him. Clearly they were **confident** that Jesus would be able to heal him.

The first question to ask is whether they accompanied their friend when Jesus led him out of the village? If present, what was their reaction when the cure was only partly effective? How did they feel when he was able to see clearly again?

THE HEALING OF THE DEAF MUTE

 Focus Passage: *Mark 7:31-37*

We should not overlook the involvement of friends in some of the healing miracles reported. For example, the four people who carried the paralysed man to the house where Jesus was teaching, determined enough that they made a hole in the roof to achieve their purpose. Friends led the blind man at Bethsaida to Jesus and pleaded on his behalf. This deaf man could 'hardly talk', so without friends he would have been unable to request healing.

There is a lesson for all of us in the action of these helpful people.

 ## Charting the action

Following his excursion into the region of Tyre and Sidon, Jesus returned to the region of Decapolis (Ten cities). While he was there, some people brought the deaf mute to him. Jesus 'took him aside, away from the crowd' (v. 33). His action of seeking privacy is reminiscent of the account of the healing of the blind man in the previous story and, as was the case there, this healing required considerable effort.

 ## Noting the emotion

The people who brought their friend to Jesus '**begged** him to place his hand on the man' (v. 32). Even though they demonstrated belief in Jesus' power, they were **overwhelmed** with **astonishment** when the cure was accomplished.

They kept talking about it even though Jesus had warned them to keep it quiet. They said 'He has done everything well' (v. 37).

Extra comment

Again we see 'spittle' used in the process of healing (see notes on the blind man of John 9, p. 59).

'There is no question of magical use here; but whether Jesus made use of spittle simply to indicate to the man that he was to expect a cure and so to awaken faith on his part, or whether he also had in mind any natural effect of the spittle, it is difficult to decide.' (C.E.B. Cranfield, *Gospel of St Mark*, Cambridge Greek Testament Commentary Series, Cambridge University Press, 1963)

'*Ephphatha!*' (see notes on healing of Jairus' daughter for comment on the use of original Aramaic, p. 74).

A CRIPPLED WOMAN HEALED

 Focus Passage: *Luke 13:10-17*

This story was one that I had overlooked entirely until I began work on the material for this book. What a story! How could I have missed it?

 Charting the action

In the congregation of one of the synagogues where Jesus was teaching was a woman 'crippled by a spirit for eighteen years'. As a result of her illness she was bent over and could not stand up straight. Jesus called her to come forward, placed his hands on her and declared, 'Woman, you are set free from your infirmity' (v. 13).

Her cure was immediate, she was able to straighten up, breaking into praise to God. We would expect that everyone witnessing this would share her jubilation. This was not the case, for the synagogue ruler was far from pleased and berated the people, 'There are six days for work, so come and be healed on those days, not on the Sabbath' (v. 14).

Jesus answered his objection by pointing out that those who owned animals such as an ox or a donkey, untied it on the Sabbath and led it out to give it water. If that was permissible, surely liberating this crippled woman should be too.

 ## Noting the emotion

Reading about the **disgruntled** attitude of the synagogue ruler, one is tempted to ask, 'What's this guy on about? Can anyone be so one-eyed?'

Notice that he does not address Jesus directly but scolds the assembled crowd for coming for healing on the wrong day. Six days are available for that sort of thing!

He is not alone in his criticism, for others present had similar attitudes. Jesus is disturbed by their **lack of compassion**, 'You hypocrites!' he thunders (v. 15).

If people were prepared to act humanely toward their oxen or their donkeys on the Sabbath, why wasn't it permissible to restore the afflicted to health? On this occasion Jesus seems to have touched their consciences. 'Jesus' words made his enemies **ashamed**. But everyone else in the crowd was **happy** about the wonderful things he was doing' (v. 17 CEV).

 ## Extra comment

A similar incident is recorded in Luke 14:1-6, where Jesus heals a man with dropsy on a Sabbath day. On that occasion he used a slightly different argument to justify his action.

'If ... a son or an ox ... falls into a well on the Sabbath day, will you not immediately pull him out?' (v. 5)

 ## For children

Explaining the difference between the Lord's day and the Sabbath is not easy, but if the children are going to understand incidents like this one, it is necessary.

HEALING THE TEN LEPERS

 Focus Passage: *Luke 17:11-19*

In modern times we understand much more about leprosy than those of earlier times. Drugs have been developed to cure it and we know it is not as contagious as once thought. In the biblical era no remedies were available and people were fearful of contamination.

Lepers were forbidden access to the towns. They carried warning bells and were required to shout to warn others of their proximity.

 ## Charting the action

Jesus was journeying in the border regions that separated Galilee from Samaria. A party of ten lepers approached him. 'They stood at a distance and shouted' their appeal for help (v. 13). Jesus instructed them to show themselves to the priests. This was the normal procedure when a leper was cured. The local priest could verify that the disease was no longer active.

Jesus put the faith of these men to the test by instructing them to act as though they had been cured. As they went they were cleansed. One of them, realising that he was healed, came back to say thank you.

 ## Noting the emotion

It seems probable that news of Jesus' presence in the area had spread. Perhaps these lepers felt there was safety in numbers rather than approaching Jesus individually. They probably came as close as they dared, calling out with a loud voice. Clearly they wanted Jesus to be aware of their presence. **Anxiety** must have turned to **exhilaration**, as following Jesus' instruction they hurried off, discovering that healing was happening. The one who returned was **jubilant**, 'praising

God in a loud voice' (v. 15). Buoyed by **joy** he 'threw himself at Jesus' feet and thanked him' (v. 16).

In Jesus' question there seems to be an expression of **disappointment**. 'Were not all ten cleansed? Where are the other nine?' (v. 17) The man is treated with compassion and dignity. 'Rise and go; your faith has made you well' (v. 19) Presumably the other nine had faith and were also healed.

 ### Extra comment

Leprosy often results in unsightly deformity due to parts deadened to feeling that become infected after injury. For example, a leper putting their hand on a stove will feel no pain because they are unaware that the stove is hot, which can result in crippling injury.

 ### For children

Because it is easy to apply the lesson on the need for gratitude, this is a popular story.

THE MEAL WITH SIMON THE PHARISEE

 Focus Passage: Luke 7:36-50

 ### Charting the action

There is limited action in this account. Jesus is invited to a meal but is ignored by his host. A woman, described as a person 'who had lived a sinful life', brings a jar of perfume and pours it on Jesus' feet. Her action prompts the conversation with Simon that followed.

Noting the emotion

Earlier, Jesus dined with a tax collector and now had an invitation from a Pharisee. The woman, probably a prostitute, would have had to muster up **courage** to enter the home of a Pharisee, who certainly would not have approved of her presence.

It was a tense moment. With copious tears the woman anointed Jesus' feet with ointment and wiped them with her hair (vv. 37,38).

Simon's reaction was to be **critical** of Jesus, though he did not openly express it. Jesus interrupted his thoughts by telling a parable about two debtors. After reciting this, he asked Simon for a judgment on which of the forgiven debtors would love the benefactor most. Simon's reply was patronising, 'I suppose the one who had the bigger debt cancelled' (v. 43). When Jesus applied the parable to him, it must have been a very humbling experience.

Then turning to the **distressed** woman, Jesus announced that her sins were forgiven (v.48).

The 'other guests' were critical of this and said to one another, 'Who is this who dares to forgive sins?' (v. 49 CEV) Ignoring their criticisms Jesus said to the woman, 'Because of your faith, you are now saved. May God give you peace!' (v. 50 CEV)

 Extra comment

The reaction of these 'other guests' is reminiscent of the scribes who were present when Jesus healed the paralytic.

'Forgiven'. What thoughts would have tumbled through the woman's mind when Jesus said this? On the outside she would have appeared restrained, but inwardly she must have been overwhelmed with **joy**.

THE WOMAN TAKEN IN ADULTERY

 Focus Passage: John 8:1-11

There is a textual problem with this passage. In the *New International Version* the heading of this section says, 'The earliest and most reliable manuscripts and other ancient writings do not have John 7:53 to 8:11.' Some modern versions leave this section out entirely. R.V.G. Tasker says: 'Scholars are agreed that this section did not originally form part of John's gospel, though it records a genuine incident in the life of Jesus.' (*John*, Tyndale New Testament Commentaries, IVP/Eerdmans, 1989)

 ## Charting the action

At dawn Jesus made his way to the Temple and was soon surrounded by a crowd who gathered to hear his teaching. Soon after, the teachers of the law and the Pharisees brought in a woman who had been caught in the act of adultery. The woman was made to stand in front of the crowd and they asked Jesus whether she should be stoned to death, which was the penalty set out in the Law of Moses (vv. 3-5).

Jesus acted 'as though he heard them not' (v. 6 AV). When they persisted he said, 'If any one of you is without sin, let him be the first to throw a stone at her' (v. 7). With that he began doodling in the sand.

He looked up shortly and found all of the accusers gone. 'Woman,' he asked, 'Where are they? Has no one condemned you?'

'No-one, sir' she said.

'Then neither do I condemn you. Go now and leave your life of sin.' (vv. 10, 11)

Noting the emotion

Identifying the emotion implicit in this story is a fascinating exercise.

The Pharisees' question is described as a trap (v. 6), so these men must have planned their move beforehand, feeling satisfied they had found a way to accuse him. If he said 'stone her' he would be in trouble with the Roman authorities. If he said 'let her go' he would be overruling the Law of Moses.

The woman must have been **distressed** as these hard-hearted men stood her in front of the crowd. When Jesus ignored their question they probably became quite **agitated**. 'They kept on questioning him' (v. 7).

We can imagine them saying:

'Aren't you going to answer us? This woman should be stoned, what are you going to say to that?' and so on. They persisted until he finally responded. Then he bent down and continued to write in the sand.

Many have speculated as to what he wrote. Was it something that reminded these men of some past actions as they were 'convicted by their own conscience'? (v. 9 AV) One by one they drifted away, 'the older ones first'. Perhaps the older ones had had more opportunities to fail than those who were younger.

The woman must have been **astonished** as each of these very vocal critics fell silent and began to slink away. Perhaps even the bystanders went too, as when Jesus finally looked up he 'saw none but the woman' (v. 10 AV).

 Extra comment

Reference to this incident occurs with some frequency in modern day secular literature. Sometimes it is used to justify adultery, but God's standards do not change. Jesus' final instruction should be noted, 'Go now and leave your life of sin' (v. 11).

THE MOUNT OF TRANSFIGURATION

Focus Passage: *Matthew 17:1-9*
Other references: *Mark 9:2-10*
                          Luke 9:28-36
                          Peter 1:16-18

  ## Charting the action

The *Contemporary English Version* entitles this section 'The True Glory of Jesus'.

Accompanied by Peter, James and John, Jesus 'went up on a very high mountain where they could be alone' (v. 1 CEV). He was changed in front of them, the report recording that his 'face shone like the sun, and his clothes became as white as the light' (v. 2). As his friends watched, Moses and Elijah appeared, 'talking with Jesus' (v. 3).

As Peter suggested that three shelters could be erected there, a bright cloud enveloped them and a voice was heard.

'This is my Son, whom I love; with him I am well pleased. Listen to him!' (v. 5)

Shortly afterward the vision faded. Jesus ordered them not to tell of their experience 'until the Son of Man has been raised from the dead' (v. 9).

  ## Noting the emotion

When the disciples saw Jesus transformed Peter suggested building the shelters because 'he did not know what to say, they were so **frightened**' (Mark 9:6). When they heard the voice speaking, they 'fell facedown to the ground, **terrified**' (v. 6).

Jesus came and touched them, 'Get up,' he said, 'Don't be afraid' (v. 7). But looking around 'they saw no one except Jesus' (v. 8).

They were **puzzled** by the instruction they were given to keep the matter to themselves and spent some time 'discussing what "rising from the dead" meant' (Mark 9:10).

 Extra comment

This experience left a lasting impression on them. Peter explains in his second letter that 'We did not follow cleverly invented stories when we told you about the power and coming of our Lord Jesus Christ, but we were eyewitnesses of his majesty' (2 Peter 1:16).

He then went on to describe the experience they shared on the mountain that day.

HEALING THE BOY WITH THE EVIL SPIRIT

 Focus Passage: *Mark 9:14-29*
Other references: Matthew 17:14-21
                        Luke 9:37-42

 Charting the action

Returning with the three from the mount of Transfiguration to the rest of his followers, Jesus found them in the middle of an argument. On enquiring about the cause of the disturbance, a man in the crowd explained that he had asked Jesus' disciples to exorcise a demon afflicting his son.

The father's description of his son's symptoms indicates a similarity to epilepsy and the boy has been described as 'the epileptic'.

Jesus ordered them to bring the boy to him. 'When the spirit saw Jesus, it immediately threw the boy into a convulsion' (v. 20). Jesus asked the father how long the boy had suffered in this way. The father answered, 'Ever since he was a child' and described some of the violent symptoms that affected the boy, appealing for help with the words, 'Please have pity and help us if you can'. Jesus replied, 'Why do you say "if you can"? Anything is possible for someone who has faith!' (vv. 21-23 CEV)

The father shouted, 'I do have faith! Please help me to have even more' (v. 24 CEV). Noticing that a larger crowd was 'running to the scene' (v. 25), Jesus turned to the boy and ordered the demon to leave him.

 Noting the emotion

There are some interesting phrases to ponder in this report indicating emotion. Jesus returned from his mountain top experience to discover the teachers of the law '**arguing**' with the disciples, while the people were '**overwhelmed with wonder** and ran to greet him'. (v. 15) Could some lingering radiance on them have caused the crowd to react like this?

When it was explained to Jesus that his disciples had unsuccessfully attempted an exorcism, Jesus seemed quite **agitated**. 'O unbelieving generation, how long shall I stay with you? How long shall I put up with you? Bring the boy to me' (v. 19).

In some of the older scripture versions it is difficult to sort out the discussion between Jesus and the father. The *Contemporary English Version* is particularly clear at this point. When the father asked Jesus to 'help us if you can', Jesus picked up the phrase 'if you can' and said in effect, 'What do you mean, **if** you can'? He had identified a degree of **doubt** in the father's request.

When Jesus rebuked the evil spirit the effect was so violent that 'the boy looked dead ... everyone said he was' (v. 26 CEV).

Picture them in your mind's eye, clustered round the inert body of the boy, each putting in their two cents worth of opinion.

Jesus took the boy's hand and helped him up. There must have been some audible **gasps** from the critics in the crowd.

Extra comment

Whether there was some lingering sense of radiance on Jesus as he returned from the mountain is thought unlikely by commentators, yet the phrase 'overwhelmed with wonder' (v. 15) seems a strong way to express surprise at his opportune arrival.

'After Jesus and the disciples had gone back home and were alone, they asked him, "Why couldn't we force out the demon." Jesus answered, "Only prayer can force out that kind of demon."' (vv. 28,29 CEV) In Mark 6:7 the disciples were given authority to exorcise demons but they had yet to learn that God's power needed to be asked for afresh.

Jesus went on to inform them of his betrayal, death and resurrection. 'But *they did not understand* what he meant and were **afraid** to ask him' (v. 32).

The father declared that he believed yet admitted to unbelief. Aren't we all a bit like that?

THE LITTLE CHILDREN AND JESUS

Focus Passage: Matthew 19:13-15
Other references: Matthew 18:1-3
                 Mark 10:13-16
                 Luke 18:15-17

I have always quite liked the old hymn, *When Mothers of Salem their children brought to Jesus,* though I am not sure how historically accurate the words are, as the town is not named in the accounts. The incident could have happened at Salem, for when Jesus left Galilee and moved into the region of Judea on the other side of the Jordan, this was approximately the location of Salem.

The second line says:

'The stern disciples drove them back and bade them to depart.' I suppose they were stern. Clearly they assumed the Lord did not need to be bothered with children at that moment. There is no suggestion that the little children were ill; the parents simply hoped that he would 'place his hands on them and pray for them' (v. 13).

Their action may have been partly motivated by superstition but their attitude reveals that they considered Jesus to be a prophet at least.

It is the next line that seems to be rather flowery:

'But Jesus saw them 'ere they fled, and sweetly smiled and kindly said, Suffer the children to come unto me.'

I think his rebuke of the disciples would have been stronger than that, while simultaneously he would be indicating to the parents that he was more than willing to accept the children.

I like the mental image that Mark gives, as he describes Jesus taking the children in his arms, putting his hands on them and blessing them (Mark 10:16).

 Extra comment

Matthew 19:14 has been the basis for wide ranging discussion in the church over many years. Exactly just what did Jesus mean when he said, 'Let the little children come to me, and do not hinder them, for the kingdom of God belongs to such as these.'

Spurgeon, a well known Baptist preacher of the 19th century said, 'I am not inclined to get away from the plain sense of that expression, not to suggest that he merely means that the kingdom consists of those who are like children. It is clear that he meant such children as those who were before him – babes and young children, of such is the kingdom of God.' He goes further in saying, 'We are convinced that all of our race who die in infancy are included in the election of grace, and partake in the redemption worked by our Lord Jesus.' (*Spiritual Parenting*, Whitaker House, 1995)

This is not the place to discuss the implication of this view at length but I recommend Ron Buckland's book *Children and God* (Scripture Union, 1988) for those wanting to pursue the subject.

THE RICH YOUNG RULER

Focus Passage: Mark 10:17-31
Other references: Matthew 19:16-30
Luke 18:18-30

  Charting the action

A young man, described by Luke as someone from the ruling classes, approached Jesus with the question, 'Good teacher, what must I do to inherit eternal life?' (v. 17)

Jesus picked up the young man's greeting and challenged it. 'Why do you call me good? No one is good – except God alone' (v. 18). In this situation Jesus did not accept the description that he was good because the young man did not recognise him as anything other than a man. His form of address was flawed, as was his question, because both were based on the false idea that eternal life is gained by effort.

Having said this, Jesus pointed to the commandments: 'If you want to enter life, obey the commandments.' 'Which ones?' asked the youth. In reply Jesus repeated the commandments that deal with personal relationships (Matthew 19:17-19).

'All these I have kept since I was a boy' is the enthusiastic reply (Mark 10:20). 'What else must I do?' (Matthew 19:20 CEV)

'Go and sell everything you own! Give the money to the poor, and you will have riches in heaven. Then come and be my follower' (Matthew 19:21 CEV). The Lord was testing the young man's priorities. He failed the test and turned away.

'It's hard for rich people to get into God's kingdom' (Mark 10:23 CEV).

 ## Noting the emotion

The young man 'ran up to Jesus and **fell on his knees** before him' (v. 17). We see from this that he was both **eager** and **humble**.

As their conversation flowed Jesus could see that the young man's desire for answers was genuine. Mark records that he 'looked at him and loved him' (v. 21). When the Lord told him to give his money away 'the man's face fell. He went away **sad**, because he had great wealth' (v. 22).

For this young man the price tag was too high. His money held first place in his life.

When Jesus explained to his disciples the difficulty the rich faced in entering the kingdom of God, the disciples were **amazed**. When Jesus used the illustration of a camel fitting through a needle's eye to explain how difficult it was, they were even **more amazed** and said to one another, 'Who then can be saved?' (v. 26)

'With man this is impossible, but not with God; all things are possible with God' (v. 27).

 ## Extra comment

In a sequel to the conversation, Peter speaks for all the disciples, 'We have left everything to follow you' (v. 28). Jesus assured him that they would benefit a hundred times. Many a missionary who has left the security and comfort of home has testified to the truth of Mark 10:29,30, affirming that they have been blessed one hundredfold.

 ## For children

As modern children are exposed to constant TV advertisements and programs suggesting that if you have got money you have 'made it', the lesson from this young man's failure is an important one for them to learn.

THE TRIUMPHAL ENTRY

Focus Passage: *Luke 19:28-44*
Other references: Matthew 21:1-11
           Mark 11: 1-11
           John 12:12-22

It was Passover time and as the feast grew closer the question on many lips was, 'What do you think? Isn't he coming to the feast at all?' (John 11:56)

Jesus had every reason to stay well away from Jerusalem at this time. Opposition against him had intensified and they were plotting 'to take his life'.

Jesus had gone into hiding and in his absence the Pharisees had 'given orders that if anyone found out where Jesus was, he should report it so that they might arrest him' (John 11:57). Not that the Pharisees had it all their own way. 'They plotted to arrest Jesus in some sly way and kill him. "But not during the Feast," they said, "or there may be a riot among the people"' (Matthew 26:4-5). This tense situation was the backdrop to the incident we have come to describe as Jesus' Triumphal Entry.

 Charting the action

The action begins with Jesus' instructions to two of his disciples to bring him an unbroken colt (vv. 28-34). If anyone objected to them untying the colt they were told to say, 'The Lord needs it.' Matthew 21:2 reports that there were two animals, a donkey and her colt, though obviously he could only sit on one of them.

As Jesus approached the city, crowds of people welcomed him, placing their cloaks on the road, cutting palm branches, which they spread on the roadway before the donkey's feet.

The crowd shouted their welcome. 'Blessed is the king who comes in the name of the Lord.' (v. 38) As the procession wound its way up into the city, Jesus was overcome with emotion and prophesied the city's destruction (vv. 41-44).

Arriving at the Temple, Jesus once again hunted the traders out and spent the next few days teaching there (vv. 45-47).

The plans of those plotting to kill him were frustrated by the enthusiasm of the people who 'hung on his words' (v. 48).

 ## Noting the emotion

Who was present in the crowd that day and what were their reactions to what was happening? Some were **bewildered** by what was happening. Their question was 'Who is this? (Matthew 21:10) Not all present could supply the answer, although the crowd had heard about the miracle of Lazarus being brought back to life. Those who had witnessed that event had been reporting it with enthusiasm (John 12: 17,18).

Some Pharisees present were **irritated** by the **enthusiasm** of the people. 'Look,' they grumbled, 'how the whole world has gone after him!' (John 12:19) Some even went as far as to complain to Jesus. 'Teacher,' they said, 'rebuke your disciples'. Jesus flatly refused to take any notice of them, 'I tell you,' he said, 'if they keep quiet, the stones will cry out' (Luke 19:39-40).

In Luke 19:41 the mood changes. Surrounded by the cheering crowd with their extravagant expressions of joy, the central character in the drama begins to **weep** openly. The reason for his tears is his knowledge of the future destruction of the city, because 'you did not recognise the time of God's coming to you' (v. 44).

Jesus' prophetic description of the destruction that was to come, when their enemies would not leave one stone upon another, was graphically fulfilled in AD70 when the Romans destroyed the city.

Josephus, the Jewish historian, reports that the devastation was so complete that no one would have recognised the formerly beautiful city. Any Jew knowing it before would have asked, 'What place is this?' Understanding this to be the city's fate, is it any wonder that Jesus wept openly?

Finally the procession reached the Temple area and the crowd dispersed. But many of the children were still swept up with the emotion of the moment and continued chanting the messianic greeting, 'Hosanna to the Son of David' (Matthew 21:15).

'Don't you hear what those children are saying?' (Matthew 21:16 CEV) The inference seems to be that Jesus should stop them but he replied, 'Yes, I do! Don't you know that the Scriptures say, "Children and infants will sing praises"?' (Matthew 21:16 CEV) Obviously he had no intention of dampening the children's enthusiasm.

 Extra comment

Matthew chapter 23 is entitled 'Seven Woes'. In it Jesus condemned in no uncertain terms the teachers of the law, describing them as 'whitewashed tombs' (v. 27), a 'brood of vipers' (v. 33) and a number of other uncomplimentary terms. Concluding with a further lament over the city of Jerusalem, 'O Jerusalem, Jerusalem, you who kill the prophets and stone those sent to you, how often I have longed to gather your children together, as a hen gathers her chicks under her wings, but you were not willing' (Matthew 23:37).

 For children

See the comments under 'Choosing the Focus' in the Introduction, p. 10.

JESUS WASHES HIS DISCIPLES' FEET

 Focus Passage: John 13:1-17

This passage opens with a remarkable statement 'Jesus knew that the time had come for him to leave this world and go to the Father. Having loved his own who were in the world, he now showed them the *full extent of his love*' (v. 1).

To understand fully this event we need to remind ourselves of a dispute that had caused friction amongst his disciples. The mother of James and John (Matthew 20:20,21) asked Jesus to permit her sons to have pride of place, one on the right, the other on the left in the kingdom (See also Matthew 19:28). Was this the mother's ambition or was she merely her sons' spokesperson? When 'the ten heard about this, they were indignant with the two brothers' (Matthew 20:24).

Aware of what was happening Jesus called them together and explained that 'whoever wants to be great among you must be your servant' (Matthew 20:26). Despite his instruction it would seem that the irritation still rankled as they gathered in that upper room.

 ## Charting the action

The evening meal was being served but there were no servants in attendance to perform the menial task of washing the dust off the travellers' feet. Clearly, none of the disciples was willing to serve the others in this way. For any one to have done so would have been to show that he realised he was the least important of those present.

Although Jesus knew that 'the Father had put all things under his power', he got up and after stripping off his outer clothing, wrapped a towel around his waist and began to wash their feet (vv. 3,4).

Noting the emotion

As Peter was not the first in the group to receive this ministration we must ask ourselves what the reaction of the others was. Were they embarrassed? Were they ashamed? It is typical of what we know of Peter's character that he should be the one to blurt out in protest. 'Lord, are *you* going to wash *my* feet?' (v. 6) Emphasising the personal pronouns 'you' and 'my' helps us to feel something of the depth of his emotion. Jesus patiently explained that Peter would understand later what his purpose was. 'No,' said Peter, '*you* shall never wash *my* feet' (v. 8). In other words, he is saying that he is not worthy to have his feet washed by one he acknowledges to be his master. 'If I don't wash you,' Jesus told him, 'you don't really belong to me' (v. 8 CEV).

Poor Peter! He is out of his depth! He cannot grasp what Jesus is saying. In desperation he says, 'Lord, don't just wash my feet. Wash my hands and my head' (v. 9 CEV). Peter has swung from one extreme to the other, finally submitting to having his feet washed. It is important to recognise that the Lord then continued to wash the feet of each disciple until he had completed the task.

After putting on his clothes again, Jesus asked them whether they understood the significance of what he had done. He explained that he had demonstrated through his action what it meant for the greater to serve the lesser. 'You call me "Teacher" and "Lord" and rightly so, for that is what I am. Now that I, your Lord and Teacher, have washed your feet, you should also wash one another's feet. I have set you an example that you should do as I have done for you' (vv. 13-15).

 Extra comment

We too are just as prone to seek position, power and prestige. The lesson the Lord sought to communicate to the disciples is as valid now as then. One of the fruits by which we will be known as his followers is our willingness to be the 'servant of all'.

THE LAST SUPPER

Focus Passage: *Luke 22:14-23*
Other references: Matthew 26:17-30
                          Mark 14:17-26

   ## Charting the action

Peter and John were instructed to prepare for the Passover meal. Jesus appears to have made secret arrangements with a house owner, possibly to prevent Judas from betraying him prematurely. They were told to look out for a man 'carrying a water jar', an action which would distinguish him in a crowd, as this was normally women's work (men carried water skins).

Following these directions they were led to a large upper room, 'all furnished', and made the necessary preparations. When the disciples were gathered together Jesus told them that he was aware that one of them planned to betray him.

When comparing the different gospel accounts, it is uncertain whether Judas left the meal before or after the distribution of the bread and the cup.

   ## Noting the emotion

When Jesus said that one of them would betray him everyone there must have been distressed. They were **all very sad**. 'Lord, you can't mean me!' (Matthew 26:22 CEV) each one of them said. As we study their reaction it becomes clear that rather than looking around at the others to see who Jesus was referring to, each disciple was inwardly conscious of his own weaknesses.

John's account differs from the other three. He records an awkward moment: 'The disciples **stared** at one another, **at a loss** to know which of them he meant' (John 13:22). At Peter's urging John asked 'Lord, who is it?' 'It is the one to whom I will give this piece of bread when I have dipped it in the dish'. John then records that he gave the bread to Judas and 'as soon as Judas took the bread *Satan entered into him*' (John 13:25-27).

 ### Extra comment

The musical *Jesus Christ SuperStar* portrays Judas more in the role of hero than as villain. In reality, it must have caused Jesus considerable distress to know that one of his intimate friends was to betray him.

After Peter makes a declaration of faith (John 6:69), Jesus openly reveals that he is aware of his betrayer. 'Have not I chosen you, the Twelve? Yet one of you is a devil!' (John 6:70) A devil! That's strong language!

John's account has an addition in brackets. ['He meant Judas, the son of Simon Iscariot, who, though one of the Twelve, was later to betray him.'] (v. 71)

When Judas is next mentioned he is objecting to Mary wasting expensive perfume, complaining that it could have been sold and the money 'given to the poor' (John 12:4). John is not deceived for he records, 'He did not say this because he cared for the poor but because he was a thief; as keeper of the money bag he used to help himself to what was put into it' (John 12:6). Money appears to be part of what motivated Judas to betray Jesus. Already he had struck a deal with the chief priests, for in anticipation of his finding a suitable moment to betray Jesus, he had received the 'thirty pieces of silver' (Matthew 26:15).

Regarding the treachery of Judas, Cranfield has this to say;

'The betrayal by one of the Twelve is a feature which would never have been created by the community. The historical worth of Mark's bald account is unquestionable.'

The final part of the Judas tragedy is played out in Matthew 27:1-10. Judas is filled with remorse and returns the money to the chief priests and elders who are indifferent to his distress. This results in Judas' suicide.

IN THE GARDEN OF GETHSEMANE

Focus Passage: *Matthew 26:36-46*
Other references: *Mark 14:32-42*
                    Luke 22:39-46

 Charting the action

Following their shared meal they went to a place called Gethsemane, at the Mount of Olives. There, taking Peter, James and John with him, Jesus moved a short distance away from the group to pray.

 Noting the emotion

How can we describe the emotions that our Lord experienced in these **terrible** moments in the Garden? Despair, desperation, disappointment are words that come to mind.

Matthew describes Jesus as **sad** and **troubled** as he contemplated the trials he knew were ahead of him. He said. 'I'm so sad that I feel as if I'm dying' (Matthew 26:38 CEV).

Moving apart from his friends his prayer reveals his **desperation**. 'My Father, if it's possible, don't make me suffer by having me drink from this cup. But do what you want, and not what I want' (v. 39 CEV).

Luke describes his **agony** as being so intense that 'his sweat was like drops of blood falling to the ground' (Luke 22:44).

When he went back to the disciples he found them asleep, '**exhausted** from **sorrow**' (Luke 22:45). It seems they shared something of his **distress**. We would not have known what he said unless they had observed him.

Mark concludes this section with Jesus facing, rather than flinching from the inevitable, with the words, 'Get up! Let's go! The one who will betray me is already here' (Mark 14:42 CEV).

 ### Extra comment

In Matthew's account of this incident, there is an interesting contrast in the wording of the prayers of Jesus that give us insight into his emotion at that time.

In his first prayer, Jesus says, 'My Father, *if it is possible*, may this cup be taken from me . . .' (26:39). After finding his disciples asleep, he returns to pray a second time, 'My Father, *if it is not possible* for this cup to be taken away . . .' (26:42). It would seem that the failure of the disciples indicated to him that his destiny was to drink 'the cup' of suffering.

JESUS PREDICTS PETER'S DENIAL

 Focus Passage: *Matthew 26:31-35*
Other references: *Mark 14:27-31*
                     Luke 22:33-38
                     John 13:31-38

 ### Charting the action

It is hard to reconcile the four separate gospel reports where Jesus predicts that his disciples will betray him, but what is clear is that he stated that all of them would fail, 'During this very night, all of you will reject me' (Matthew 26:31 CEV).

Extra comment

The whole group immediately became **defensive** and Peter, always the more **outspoken**, is adamant that Jesus is wrong. 'Even if all fall away on account of you, I never will' (v. 33). Only a short time before Peter declared, 'you shall never wash my feet' (John 13:8) then had to back down. Now Peter is at it again! He is slow to learn. Having said that they will reject him that very night, Jesus prophesies Peter's three-fold denial and even gives a time limit for this, before the crowing of the rooster.

In his reply, Peter not only repeats his claim that he will never disown his Lord but repeats it with even greater emphasis, 'Even if I have to die with you' (v. 35). Mark reports that Peter '**insisted emphatically**'. Peter is not the only one, for 'all the other disciples said the same' (14:31).

THE ARREST OF JESUS

 Focus Passage: *John 18:1-11*
Other references: *Matthew 26:47-56*
                     Mark 14:43-52
                     Luke 22:47-53

All four of the gospels report this incident and each has a slightly different account of what happened. Obviously, the arrest took place at night, as the detachment of soldiers carried torches, lanterns, swords and clubs. It would appear they were expecting some resistance.

 Charting the action

Judas Iscariot had at last found the means of carrying out the deal he made with the chief priests, thus earning the money already paid to him. He knew where Jesus was likely to be for 'Jesus had often met there with his disciples' (John 18:2).

Walking up to Jesus, he kissed him in greeting, the signal pre-arranged with the soldiers, who now arrested Jesus. One of the disciples, whom John identifies as Peter, drew a sword and made a wild swipe with it, cutting off the ear of Malchus, the servant of the High Priest. Jesus then ordered Peter to put his sword away and touched the man's wounded ear, healing it.

 ## Noting the emotion

Each gospel gives a different account of what happened. Matthew reports that Judas went up to Jesus saying, 'Greetings, Rabbi', then kissed him. Jesus replies with, 'Friend, do what you came for' (Matthew 26:49,50). In Luke, Jesus is reported as saying, 'Judas, are you betraying the Son of Man with a kiss?' (Luke 22:48) while John says that Jesus approached the squad with the question, 'Who is it you want?' 'Jesus of Nazareth', they replied. 'I am he', Jesus said. When he said this 'they drew back and fell to the ground' (John 18:4-6)

This is one of the most dramatic moments in the whole of the gospel record. What was it about Jesus that **terrified** his enemies at that moment? Peter, true to character thought the matter could be resolved by **fighting,** but Jesus instantly **rebuked** him for his action, then surrendered himself to the squad.

Panic suddenly gripped Jesus' followers and they all 'ran off and left him' (Mark 14:50).

PETER DISOWNS JESUS

Focus Passage: *Matthew 26:69-75*
Other references: *Mark 14:66-72*
                             Luke 22:54-62
                             John 18:15-27

Charting the action

As Jesus predicted, when he was arrested 'all the disciples deserted him and fled' (Matthew 26:56). However, Peter and 'another disciple' (John 18:15, therefore probably John) drifted back, following 'at a distance' (Mark 14:54).

Jesus was taken to the high priest's house. Because this other disciple was known to the high priest he was able to enter the courtyard, 'but Peter had to wait outside at the door' (John 18:16). The other disciple came back and spoke to the girl on duty at the door, and brought Peter into the courtyard where he joined a group sitting by a fire.

Noting the emotion

Luke describes a servant girl subjecting Peter to close scrutiny, 'she looked closely at him' when she saw him in the courtyard. 'This man was with him', she declared (Luke 22:56). Peter brushed her remark aside, 'I don't know what you are talking about' (Matthew 26:70).

A short time later someone else made a similar claim, 'This fellow was with Jesus of Nazareth' (v. 71). This time, Peter's denial becomes more emphatic – 'He denied it again, **with an oath**' (v. 72).

Listening to Peter's denials, someone else in the group gathered around the fire observed, 'Surely you are one of them, for your accent gives you away' (v. 73), bringing an outburst of protest from Peter. 'He began to **call down curses** on himself and he swore to them, "I don't know the man!"' (v. 74) He could not be more emphatic than that.

'Immediately a cock crowed' – 'immediately' – as though the cock had waited for his cue to crow (v. 74).

It is difficult to know exactly where Jesus was at this moment, but it is clear the two made eye contact. Luke reports that the Lord turned and looked straight at Peter (Luke 22:61). The memory of Jesus' warning flooded back to Peter and he broke down and **'wept bitterly'** (v. 75).

 Extra comment

If you have ever felt ashamed for failing to openly confess your allegiance to the Lord Jesus, you will understand something of Peter's feelings at that moment.

John adds an interesting piece of information about one of Peter's accusers, 'a relative of the man whose ear Peter had cut off', saying 'Didn't I see you with him in the olive grove?' (John 18:26) In the face of that kind of evidence, Peter's denial needed to be pretty strong.

JESUS BEFORE THE SANHEDRIN

 Focus Passages: John 18:12-24
Matthew 26:57-67
Other reference: Mark 14:53-65

To cover the whole episode of Jesus' trial before the Sanhedrin it is necessary to consult John first, as he indicates that Jesus was taken first before Annas, an ex high priest, and the father-in-law of Caiaphas, the current holder of that office. Matthew and Mark give insights into the second part of the trial, held before Caiaphas.

Charting the action

After his arrest, Jesus was bound and led to Annas who questioned him 'about his disciples and his teaching.' When Jesus protested that his preaching had been done openly, 'one of the officials struck him in the face' (John 18:19,22). 'If I have done something wrong, say so. But if not, why did you hit me?' (John 18:23 CEV)

Jesus was then sent on to Caiaphas, seen to be eager to find some charge that could be used to accuse Jesus before the Roman authorities. When Jesus refused to answer questions (Mark 14:61), Caiaphas challenged him to state openly whether he was the Messiah, the Son of the glorious God' (Mark 14:62 CEV). When Jesus admitted this, the Sanhedrin gave its ruling – Jesus was 'worthy of death' (Mark 14:64).

 Noting the emotion

As we look at this incident it is obvious that a number of people became very **agitated**.

My mental picture of the trial before Caiaphas is that of a confusing hubbub with everyone talking at once, as the chief priests and the whole Sanhedrin 'were looking for false evidence against Jesus so they could put him to death' (Matthew 26:59).

Mark records that some stood up and gave this 'false testimony' (Mark 14:56). Examine the next sentence. In what way was their evidence 'false'? 'We heard him say, "I will destroy this man-made temple and in three days will build another, not made by man"' (Mark 14:58).

Jesus refused to discuss this and Caiaphas went on to ask Jesus if he was Christ. His answer, that indeed he was, inflamed Caiaphas, who became **very vocal**, tearing his clothes to demonstrate his **annoyance** and **anger** (Mark 14:63).

Following this, the situation became **violent**. People spat at Jesus and hit him with their fists. Mark added that the guards joined in and beat him too. (v. 65) To followers of Jesus, it must have been a distressing scene.

 Extra comment

I have been under the impression that under Roman rule the Jews did not have the right to put a person to death. However, commentators suggest that the Jews could have executed Jesus by stoning, without reference to Pilate. They suggest that the Jewish leaders wanted Jesus to die a death (such as crucifixion) that would be under the curse of the law. (See Deuteronomy 21:23, 'anyone who is hung on a tree is under God's curse.') Paul picks up this train of thought in his letter to the Galatians: 'Christ redeemed us from the curse of the law by becoming a curse for us, for it is written: Cursed is everyone who is hung on a tree' (Galatians 3:13).

 For children

When I refer children back to the story of Jesus hunting the traders from the Temple (John 2:12-22), where the basis of these accusations against Jesus is found (v. 19), they never fail to amaze me with their ability to discern that the accusations made to Caiaphas are false. What Jesus is inferring stresses not the words 'I will', but the unspoken words, '[*If you*] destroy this temple . . . in three days I will build it again' (v. 19, CEV).

THE TRIAL BEFORE PILATE

Focus Passage: John 18:28—19:16
Other references: Matthew 27:11-31
                           Mark 15:1-20
                           Luke 23:1-25

Charting the action

After a long night, 'at daybreak' (Luke 23:66), Jesus was led off to face Pilate, the Roman Governor.

On arrival, the Jews did not enter the palace because they would want to 'avoid ceremonial uncleanness' (John 18: 28) to prevent their exclusion from the Passover meal. Thus it was necessary for Pilate to come out to the Jews rather than have them come to him. This was hardly likely to put Pilate in the best of moods, as his blunt demand, 'What charges are you bringing against this man?' reveals (v. 29).

Perhaps they expected Pilate to be overawed by their numbers and dignity, as their answer also betrays a degree of irritation. 'If he were not a criminal we would not have handed him over to you' (v. 30). This is too vague a statement for Pilate, who attempts to dismiss them with his haughty reply, 'Take him yourselves and judge him by your own law' (v. 31). To reply to this, they are forced to admit their subordination to the power of Rome. 'But we have no right to execute anyone' (v. 31; even if the Jews had been permitted to stone Jesus, John notes that this would have been contrary to God's purpose, v. 32.)

It was probably at this point that the Jews brought out their threefold accusation against Jesus.

• We have found this man subverting our nation.
• He opposes payment of taxes to Caesar.
• He claims to be Christ, a King (Luke 23:2).

Pilate was not hoodwinked for a moment. Re-entering the judgment hall he ignored the first two accusations, focusing on the third of these claims. He asked Jesus, 'are you the King of the Jews?' (John 18:33)

If he had answered 'yes' or 'no', this would have confused the matter, so Jesus answered Pilate's question with another, 'Is that your own idea or did others talk to you about me?' (John 18:34)

Pilate's tone of reply, 'Do you think I am a Jew?' betrays contempt. ' It was your own people and your chief priests who handed you over to me. What is it you have done?' (John 18:35)

Jesus ignored this question too, returning to the question of his kingship. In the conversation that followed Jesus admitted that he had come to be a king (John 18:33-37).

Pilate returned to the delegation outside the door and gave his verdict, 'I find no basis for a charge against this man' (Luke 23:4). But the Jews were not ready to accept any verdict but the death sentence. They were insistent. 'He stirs up the people all over Judea by his teaching. He started in Galilee and has come all the way here' (Luke 23:5).

Pilate pricked up his ears at the mention of Galilee, for Galilee was Herod's jurisdiction. When he ordered them to take Jesus to Herod, was Pilate hoping to pass the responsibility of sentencing Jesus on to someone else? But sending Jesus to Herod proved to be little more than a deviation to the main plot, as Jesus was returned without any statement of charges that could be substantiated. Pilate was forced to face Jesus' accusers again: 'You brought me this man as one who was inciting the people to rebellion. I have examined him in your presence and have found no basis for your charges against him. Neither has Herod, for he sent him back to us; as you can see he has done nothing to deserve death. Therefore, I will punish him and then release him.' (Luke 23:14-16).

It is ironic that Pilate, despite his declaration that Jesus was innocent, was prepared to have Jesus whipped (Luke 23:16). This in itself was no light punishment.

When Pilate indicated that he would release Jesus, the Jewish protestations reached fever pitch, 'With one voice they cried out, "Away with this man!"' (Luke 23:19). At this point it appears that Pilate offered an alternative: the release of either Jesus or Barabbas.

The crowd made its demands clear: Barabbas should be released and Jesus crucified. Then Pilate ordered Jesus to be flogged. Later, Jesus was paraded before the crowd wearing 'the crown of thorns and the purple robe ... Here is the man', announced Pilate, expressing contempt (John 19:5). In effect he was saying, 'Here he is – the poor fellow. Would such a caricature of a king be a danger either to Israel or Rome?' (R.V.G. Tasker, *John*, Tyndale New Testament Commentaries, IVP, 1989)

The clamour in the crowd broke out with renewed vigour, 'Crucify! Crucify!'

'You take him and crucify him. As for me I find no basis for a charge against him' (John 19:6).

 ### Noting the emotion

Both the action and the emotion of this mock trial are so interwoven that it is impossible to separate them.

When first approached by the delegation of the Jews, Pilate was **contemptuous** both of the delegation, and of the pathetic looking prisoner they had brought before him.

Remember Jesus had been interrogated and mistreated throughout the previous night so anyone looking less like a king would be hard to imagine. How ironic when the accusers said that Jesus claimed to be a king. Pilate's tone seems to reveal his contempt: 'Are you the king of the Jews?' (John 18:33)

Little by little, events of those few hours **shattered Pilate's self-confidence**.

At what point the message from his wife arrived is hard to ascertain, but her words, 'Don't have anything to do with that innocent man. I have had nightmares because of him', probably made him uneasy (Matthew 27:19 CEV).

After exhausting every avenue available to him, including the offer to release one of the prisoners, Pilate still maintained that he found no reason to condemn Jesus. At this point the Jews' **real accusation** finally **surfaced**: 'We have a law, and according to that law he must die, because he claimed to be the Son of God' (John 19:7).

'When Pilate heard this he was **even more afraid**' (John 19:8).

Consider this verse with care. It is the key to understanding much of what will follow here.

It indicates that he was already **fearful**. Perhaps the letter from his wife troubled him, but now as a result of the accusation that Jesus claimed to be the Son of God, Pilate is greatly disturbed as the subsequent dialogue reveals. Very likely his tone is much gentler, as he asks with a sense of awe, 'Where do you come from?' (John 19:9) Does he sense that Jesus' claim to be the Son of God may be the truth?

This question of Pilate's is one of the most important questions a person can ask. To know where Jesus comes from is to know the most important thing about him.

When Jesus remained silent Pilate said, 'Don't you know that I have the power to let you go free or to nail you to a cross?' (John 19:10 CEV) Jesus then declared to Pilate that he was only an instrument, 'the one who handed me over to you is guilty of a greater sin' (v. 11).

It is unclear whether this statement refers to Judas or to Caiaphas (cf. with John 18:35).

'From then on, Pilate tried to set Jesus free' (v. 12). What prevented him was the implied threat that the Jews would report him to Caesar. 'If you let this man go, you are no friend of Caesar' (v. 12).

On a previous occasion when Jewish leaders came to Pilate, his high handed action resulted in an official complaint to Tiberius, the Roman Caesar and Pilate was reprimanded by him. Pilate had no wish to repeat this experience. The threat by the Jewish leaders was what finally broke

Pilate's resistance and he 'decided to grant their demand' (Luke 23:24).

Pilate could not resist enjoying a joke at the Jews' expense. His words, 'Here is your king', as he paraded Jesus before the crowd, was greeted with the full-throated roar from the crowd, 'Take him away! Take him away! Crucify him!'

'Shall I crucify your king?' Pilate asked.

'We have no king but Caesar' (John 19:15).

What an incredible statement! The Jews hated the Romans intensely, yet here they are asserting allegiance to the Caesar they despised. In the mouth of a worshipper of the God of Israel these words were blasphemy.

Pilate plays one last scene in this unfolding drama. Ordering a bowl of water, when his attendants bring this to him, he washes his hands in front of the crowd: 'I am innocent of this man's blood' he said, 'It is your responsibility!' (Matthew 27:24)

Their reply was terrifying. 'Let his blood be on us and on our children!' (27:26)

Then finally, Pilate handed him over to be crucified.

 ## Extra comment

Working through these gripping chapters, one of the things standing out is **the silence** of Jesus in a number of situations. The chief priests accused him of many things then once again Pilate asked him, '"Aren't you going to answer? See how many things they are accusing you of." But Jesus still made no reply, and Pilate **was amazed**.' (Mark 15:3-5)

Herod was **greatly pleased** when Pilate sent Jesus to him. 'He plied him with many questions, but Jesus gave him no answer' (Luke 23:9).

Here again Jesus maintained a dignified silence even though surrounded by many of the chief priests and teachers of the law who were **accusing** him **vehemently**.

Pilate's question, 'Where do you come from?' (John 19:9) was also met with silence.

Matthew, Mark and Luke report Pilate's offer to release Barabbas, but it is Mark who suggests that the request for the release of a prisoner came from the people themselves (15:11). Barabbas, described by Matthew as a 'notorious prisoner' (Matthew 27:16), was involved in an insurrection which led to some murders. Because of his reputation as one of the worst of criminals, was probably the reason Pilate selected him as the alternative choice.

Little did Pilate know that the priests and elders were busy persuading the crowd to choose Barabbas, so he would have been most surprised when Barabbas rather than Jesus was chosen as the person to be freed.

 For children

We cannot be faithful to the gospel record without reporting the story of Jesus' trial and crucifixion. However, for children, I prefer to focus on the rejection Jesus endured, rather than concentrating on and vividly recounting the physical suffering of the crown of thorns, the nails in his hands and feet, the spear in his side, etc.

THE CRUCIFIXION

 Focus Passages: *Matthew 27:32-56*
Mark 15:21-41
Luke 23:26-49
John 19:17-27
Other reference: *1 Peter 2:23*

It is now years since I was first appointed a children's missioner of Scripture Union's Children's Special Service Mission. My responsibility in this role was to conduct after school children's missions throughout the state of New South Wales. When I commenced my task, my boss, the Reverend Basil Williams said, 'Here you are boy, you might find these useful!' and handed me a bundle of long galley proof sheets. These were the proofs of a book entitled *To Teach Others Also*, by a long serving children's missioner, Hudson Pope, which was in the process of production.

Studying these sheets eagerly, in the weeks that followed I applied many of the principles he outlined. One of the things I took to heart, which I have applied ever since was:

'You will be wise often to tell the story of the crucifixion. Its telling will bring a hush over almost any audience; there is a strange fascination about it. He became obedient unto death, even the death of the cross.'

 ## Charting the action

'The soldiers led Jesus away' (Mark 15:16). Jesus had already suffered abuse in the high priest's house, and from Herod and his soldiers (Luke 23:11), now this intensified as a whole company of soldiers gathered round him, and made fun of him (Matthew 27:27-31). By the time they led him out to crucify him. Jesus was so exhausted that he was unable to carry the cross. The soldiers commandeered the help of Simon, described as the father of Alexander and Rufus (Mark 15:21). It is possible that Alexander and Rufus were Christians. Rufus may be the same person mentioned in Romans 16:13.

Arriving at the Place of the Skull, Jesus was offered 'some wine mixed with a drug to ease the pain, but he refused to drink it' (Mark 15:23 CEV).

Two suggestions as to why he refused have been proposed; it may have been due to the vow he made in Mark 14:25, or because he was determined to avoid nothing of 'the cup' which his Father had given him (Mark 14:36).

Pilate had a notice prepared and fastened to the cross that read 'Jesus of Nazareth, the King of the Jews' (John 19:19). The Jews attempted to have this changed, but without success.

Three hours later 'darkness came over the whole land'. This eerie darkness lasted for a period of three hours, after which Jesus cried with a loud voice:

'*Eloi, Eloi, lama sabachthani?*' (Mark 15:34)

Shortly afterwards 'Jesus breathed his last' (Mark 15:37). At that moment the 'curtain in the temple was torn in two from top to bottom' (Mark 15:38).

Meanwhile, a delegation approached Pilate with the request that the death of the prisoners be speeded up, by breaking their legs. Permission was granted but when it was discovered that Jesus was already dead, 'one of the soldiers pierced Jesus' side with a spear, bringing a sudden flow of blood and water' (John 19:34).

 ## Noting the emotion

The emotion of the soldiers

Anyone who has had to endure **ridicule** from a crowd will have a glimmer of understanding of the **mockery** Jesus endured from the soldiers. What comes to mind is a large group of men all trying to outdo each other in heaping abuse on the pathetic figure of their prisoner.

Once the crucifixion procession began, the soldiers would have fulfilled their part with **ruthless** competency. We do not know whether Simon dared to protest when they forced him to carry the cross. Nailing someone to a cross, even though it was an action of incredible brutality, was all part of the day's work for a soldier.

Unconcerned with his suffering, they turned their attention to the question of who would commandeer his clothing. His undergarment is described as 'woven in one piece' and they decided that the most sensible thing to do was to cast lots for it. The soldier who won it must have felt the day turned out to be profitable for him! (John 19:23,24)

When Jesus gave the cry '*Eloi, Eloi, lama, sabachthani*', one man, probably a soldier, showed glimmer of compassion, by offering him some wine vinegar (Mark 15:36).

At the moment of his death the indifference of the soldiers was shattered when 'the earth shook and the rocks split' (Matthew 27:51). 'When the centurion and those with him who were guarding Jesus saw the earthquake and all that had happened they were terrified' (Matthew 27:54). The centurion was moved to say, 'Surely this man was the Son of God!' (Mark 15:39)

The emotion of the crowd

The vultures were there! The chief priests, the leaders and the teachers of the Law of Moses also made fun of Jesus. It would appear that they did not address him directly but talked about him to one another. They said, 'He saved others, but he can't save himself' (Matthew 27:41-42). This statement was probably accompanied by **raucous laughter**. Their words are quite an admission, 'he saved others'.

Once more they demand a miraculous sign: 'Let him come down now from the cross and we will believe in him' (Matthew 27:43; cf. John 6:30 and Mark 8:11).

Passers by joined in the **mockery** 'hurling insults' at him, reminding Jesus of his words at the cleansing of the Temple, 'You who are going to destroy the temple and build it in three days, save yourself' (Matthew 27:40).

As you tell the story you need to reflect the tone of their ridicule.

The darkness and the earthquake made them change their tune, 'they beat their breasts and went away' (Luke 23:48).

The emotion of Jesus' friends

Despite the fact that most of his disciples had fled, 'a large number of people followed him, including women who **mourned** and **wailed** for him' (Luke 23:27).

Some of these are identified as his mother, his mother's sister, Mary the wife of Clopas and Mary Magdalene. 'The disciple whom he loved (John's way of describing himself) was standing near by' (John 19:25,26).

We can only speculate as to what Mary must have been feeling as Simeon's prophecy (Luke 2:35) found its fulfilment.

The emotion of the two thieves

In some respects these men are minor players in this great drama. They participate in a brief scene only. We know little about them except their reason for being there.

When we compare the different accounts, we discover that to begin with 'the robbers who were crucified with him also heaped insults on him', probably through gritted teeth (Matthew 27:44).

For some reason, one of them changed his opinion, rebuking his fellow thief, 'Don't you fear God, since you are under the same sentence? We are punished justly, for we are getting what our deeds deserve, but this man has done nothing wrong' (Luke 23:40-41).

What do you think brought about this change which led to a strong appeal to Jesus and a wonderful promise?

The emotion of Jesus

Peter identifies for us the reaction of Jesus to all that happened on that terrible day. 'When they hurled their insults at him, he did not retaliate; when he suffered, he made no threats. Instead, he entrusted himself to him who judges justly' (1 Peter 2:23). As the cruel nails were hammered home Jesus prayed for those who were doing it 'Father, forgive them for they do not know what they are doing' (Luke 23:34)

Despite his **suffering** Jesus revealed **concern** for his mother's welfare, making a request of John that he would care for her (John 19:26-27).

The moment of his cry; 'My God, My God, why have you forsaken me?' (Mark 15:33) revealed the deepest **anguish** of all. This was the cup he feared to drink (Mark 14:36) and we should understand it in the light of 2 Corinthians 5:21 and Galatians 3:13. Once that moment was past it was followed by a triumphant shout. The hymn writer expressed it this way:

Lifted up was he to die
'It is finished' was his cry
Now in heav'n exalted high
Hallelujah! what a saviour.

 ### Extra comment

The cry from the cross, '*Eloi, Eloi, lama, sabachthani*', needed to be recorded in its original language in the English translations, or the discussion that followed that referred to Elijah would be unintelligible.

 ### For children

Easter, like the Christmas story, needs to be approached with a different focus (see Introduction). Here are some suggestions for those working with older primaries or young teens.

Witnesses
Motivation – discuss the role of different types of witnesses in a criminal trial. Character witnesses may be called to testify as to the good character of the accused, usually the person's friends.

Introduce five witnesses to Jesus' character (mostly his enemies) and report what they said about him. Judas Iscariot, Matthew 27:3. Pilate's wife, Matthew 27:19. Pilate, Luke 23:14, the penitent thief, Luke 23:41 and the centurion, Luke 23:47.

In conclusion explain that the innocent man gave his life for the guilty.

This outline can be enhanced with flash card pictures of the hands of the five witnesses in appropriate poses.

Soldiering on
Motivation: This could be a first person interview with a regular soldier in the Roman occupying army at the time of Jesus' death. The soldier could detail his experience as
• a member of the squad which arrested Jesus

- one of the group on duty at the crucifixion
- one of the guards who fled in terror from the tomb of Jesus who was bribed to say that the disciples had stolen the body.

If the governor hears
Present the story in the first person through the eyes of an attendant in Pilate's palace. He could trace the events from the time Pilate gave the order for the crucifixion reporting the interruptions.

- the delegation requesting the change of the sign on the cross (John 19:21)
- the delegation requesting the deaths to be hastened (John 19:31)
- Joseph requesting the body of Jesus (John 19:38)
- the delegation to have the tomb secured (Matthew 27:64)
  The conclusion could centre on Matthew 28:14.

THE BURIAL OF JESUS

Focus Passage: *Matthew 27:57-66*
Other references: *Mark 15:42-47*
                            Luke 23:50-56
                            John 19:38-42
                            Corinthians 15:4

 ## Charting the action

When Jesus died, Joseph of Arimathea approached Pilate for permission to bury his body. 'Pilate was **surprised** to hear that he was already dead' (Mark 15:43,44) and sent for the centurion, who verified the truth of Joseph's claim. After being given permission, Joseph, with the help of Nicodemus, took the body of Jesus and after wrapping it in linen 'he placed it in his own new tomb' (Matthew 27:60).

Presumably if they had had more time they would have chosen to bury him elsewhere (see John 19:42). This activity was observed by some of the women (Luke 23:49).

 Noting the emotion

- What insights into the character of the people involved can we find here?
- First there is Joseph, a member of the Council (the Sanhedrin). He is described as a 'good and upright man who had not consented to their decision and action' (Luke 23:50-51). Joseph had been a secret disciple but now by his action, he openly declares his allegiance to Jesus (John 19:38).
- Then Nicodemus once again steps on to centre stage. It seems obvious from his display of devotion in bringing such a large quantity of the expensive spices myrrh and aloes to prepare Jesus' body for burial, that he too is now declaring which side he is on (John 19:39).
- Finally, the women, in particular Mary Magdalene and Mary the mother of James and Joses, were watching (Matthew 27:55,56). They would not have presumed to offer to help two such important members of the Council but 'stood at a distance, watching these things' (Luke 23:49). After marking the location of the tomb, they returned home to prepare spices and ointment for the embalming of the body. It cannot seriously be suggested that on their return two days later, they went to the wrong tomb.

 Extra comment

Matthew is the only writer to report the subsequent visit to Pilate by the chief priests and Pharisees the following day. They requested the tomb be sealed and a guard posted there. Their reason for asking is enlightening. 'Sir,' they said, 'we remember that while he was still alive that deceiver said, "After three days I will rise again"' (Matthew 27:63).

If you check the record, as I have already mentioned, you will discover that he did not make such a statement. He did however hint about this in John 2:19 when the traders were chased from the Temple, and also in Matthew 12:38-40, when in response to their persistent demand for a miraculous sign, he referred to 'the sign of the prophet Jonah. For as Jonah was three days and three nights in the belly of a huge fish, so the Son of Man will be three days and three nights in the heart of the earth.'

Although Pilate granted the necessary permission (Matthew 27:65,66), it proved to be a futile exercise.

THE RESURRECTION

 Focus Passage: *John 20:1-18*
Other references: *Matthew 28:1-10*
Mark 16:1-14
Luke 24:1-12

Memory is a funny thing. As I sat and thought about the resurrection, my mind flashed back to a conversation of many years ago. At the time, I was milking a cow while my friend lounged against the shed wall.

'What would you say is the most important thing about the Christian faith?' he asked

'Jesus died for my sins upon the cross,' was my confident reply.

'No! You're wrong! The resurrection of Jesus is the central truth.'

Of course, I could see that he was absolutely right. What value did any belief in forgiveness of sins have if Jesus did not rise from the dead?

It is our certainty that Jesus is risen that gives us hope.

Charting the action

First there was a 'violent earthquake' followed by the arrival of an angel at the tomb, who 'rolled back the stone and sat on it' (Matthew 28:2).

When the women arrived at the tomb on that first Easter morning they discovered that the guards were in shock (v. 4) and the body of Jesus was gone (v. 6). They reported this to the disciples (v. 8) and Peter and John ran to the tomb to investigate (Luke 24:12, John 20:2,3). The guards went to the chief priests to report what happened (v. 11).

 Noting the emotion

The emotion of the guards

In all the gospel records, whenever humans are confronted with the appearance of an angel, they are **terrified**. The guards appointed to protect the grave of Jesus were no exception. 'The guards were so **afraid** of him that they shook and became like dead men' (Matthew 28:4).

The emotion of the women

On their way to the tomb the women were **worrying** over a perceived difficulty, 'Who will roll the stone away from the entrance of the tomb?' (Mark 16:3)

On arrival they discovered to their **surprise** that the stone was already rolled away from the tomb. Luke reports that they entered the tomb but they did not find the body of the Lord Jesus. 'While they were **wondering** about this, suddenly two men in clothes that gleamed like lightening stood beside them' (Luke 24:2-4).

Frightened they 'bowed down with their faces to the ground.' 'Why do you look for the living among the dead? He is not here; he has risen' (Luke 24:5-6).

The emotion of the disciples

I can recall telling the story of the resurrection to a group of children and quizzing them the following day on what they had learned.

'When the women came to the disciples and reported that the grave of Jesus was empty', I asked, 'what did they do?'

I pointed to one of the girls with her hand up. She stood up, screwed up her face and said, 'Erhah'.

I looked at her with astonishment, then realised that this was how I had told the story. I had not told them that the disciples had treated the report as nonsense, but had depicted their response with a sneer.

The first reaction of the disciples to the news of Jesus' resurrection was **unbelief**. Luke reports, 'they **did not believe** the women, because their words seemed to them like **nonsense**' (24:11). But despite their scepticism they decided to check it out for themselves.

Peter and John both ran to the tomb, with John arriving first, hesitating to enter. Peter, the more impetuous, did not hesitate but plunged in. He noticed the way the shroud lay and that the cloth that had been around Jesus' head was folded up by itself. John then followed and after observing these things, 'He saw and believed' (John 20:3-8).

 Extra comment

Another pointer to the authenticity of the gospel record is the prominence given to the women's story. They were courageous when all the others 'forsook him and fled'. They were the first to visit the empty tomb, the first to tell the message of his resurrection and Mary Magdalene, the first to see the risen Lord. If the writings were mythical you would not expect to find these features in the gospel records, as the opinions of women did not amount to much in those days.

Trying to reconcile the four gospel accounts is a bewildering task, as many of the details do not fit. Matthew refers to 'an angel of the Lord', Mark describes 'a young man in a white robe', Luke refers to 'two men in clothes that gleamed like lightning' and John reports 'two angels in white'.

If you compare the accounts of a modern day event in two or more newspapers, you will discover considerable differences between them. Rather than causing alarm, the conflicting reports should give us confidence that these people were reporting the event as they remembered it.

As the storyteller, while it is important to be aware of these variations, it is wise to concentrate on only one account, if you wish to avoid confusion in the minds of the audience.

MARY MAGDALENE SEES JESUS

 Focus Passage: *John 20:10-18*

Mary Magdalene had every reason for her unswerving devotion to the Lord Jesus as she had been cured from demon possession (Luke 8:2). She and a number of other women travelled with the apostolic band and helped support them 'out of their own means' (Luke 8:3).

Mary accompanied Jesus' mother to Golgotha where they witnessed his crucifixion (John 19:25) and lingered behind after the crowd dispersed, watching to see where Jesus' body was taken for burial (Mark 15:47).

 ## Charting the action

When describing the events of Easter morning, the only person John mentions as present at the empty tomb is Mary Magdalene. He tells how she hurried off to tell the disciples the news about what she found there.

After Peter and John visited the tomb Mary lingered behind after they returned home. Then, because she was in the right place at the right time, she had a personal meeting with her risen Lord.

 Noting the emotion

Mary's emotion changed from **deep distress** to **elation** when confronted by Jesus. The person she least expected to meet was the risen Lord, so when he first appeared she mistook him for the gardener. Through her tears she sobbed out her request, 'Sir, if you have taken his body away, please tell me, so I can go and get him' (John 20:15 CEV).

'Mary!' He did not need to say another word. Recognition was instantaneous.

'Master!' she exclaimed and rushed toward him. He prevented her from touching him, telling her to tell his brothers that 'I am returning to my Father and your Father, to my God and your God' (John 20:17). She then hurried off with the news.

What an **exciting** moment it must have been when she burst in with the announcement, 'I have seen the Lord!' (John 20:18).

THE MEETING ON THE EMMAUS ROAD

 Focus Passage: *Luke 24:13-35*

A 'Christian Brethren' assembly purchased land and established a house party campsite in French's Forest Sydney. The road leading to their property had never been named so they approached their local council to have it registered as 'Emmaus Road'. Their request was approved and the appropriate sign erected. In conversation, one of the long time local residents said, 'I dunno what you blokes have got that we haven't. We've been trying to get this road named for years. It must have been that good aboriginal name you picked.'

 ## Charting the action

Emmaus is described as a village 'about 12 kilometres from Jerusalem' (v. 13 CEV).

Cleopas and his companion were on their way home and were discussing the reports given of the events in Jerusalem. Jesus caught up with them but they did not recognise him.

As they journeyed they chatted together about what had happened and what it all meant, until finally they reached their destination. They persuaded Jesus to stay with them as it was late. When he blessed and broke the bread they recognised him. Hurrying back to Jerusalem to share their experience with other disciples, they then learnt that the Lord had appeared to Peter as well.

 ## Noting the emotion

The men were mooching along the road. They were in no hurry. What was the point? Their future looked bleak. All their **hopes** had been **dashed** when they saw their leader die.

An imaginary conversation could have gone like this:

'What gets me is why he went to Jerusalem in the first place. He knew there would be trouble.'

'Yes, I'm sure he knew, but he was determined to go.'

'Well, what happens now? It's the end of any plans he may have had.'

'What puzzles me is this report that his grave is empty.'

'Oh, beats me. The women must have been seeing things.'

Luke reports that they were 'talking about everything that had happened' (v. 14). The storyteller could invent a conversation like this, providing it came within the limits of the events that actually took place.

When Jesus approached them and questioned them about their conversation, 'they stood still, their faces **downcast**' (v. 17). They must have been very **dejected**.

Cleopas asked, 'Are you the only person from Jerusalem who doesn't know what was happening there these last few days?' (v. 18 CEV)

The bluntness of these words implied that the questioner had to be pretty dumb if he did not know what had been going on in Jerusalem. There was a touch of irony too, for Cleopas was asking the only person who really did know what had been happening.

'What do you mean?' Jesus asked (v. 19 CEV).

Their reply revealed something of their hopes, 'we **had hoped** that he was the one who was going to redeem Israel' and something of their **confusion** as they recounted the news the women had brought them.

Jesus' rebuke, 'how foolish you are', seems very direct for a person thought to be a stranger, but twelve kilometres was a long enough distance which would have given Jesus ample time to explain 'what was said in all the Scriptures concerning himself' (vv. 25,27).

By the time they reached their destination they were eager to continue the relationship and 'urged him strongly' to stay with them (v. 29).

When recognition dawned on them after he had given the blessing and broken the bread, they said to one another, 'Were not our hearts **burning within us** while he talked with us on the road and opened the Scriptures to us?' (v. 32)

What an **excited** gathering it must have been when they returned to Jerusalem to find their friends bubbling over with joy at the news that the risen Lord had appeared to Peter. Then telling their story, they had scarcely finished when Jesus appeared amongst them (vv. 33-36).

We would expect there to be jubilation, but instead they were '**startled** and frightened, thinking they saw a ghost' (v. 37).

Jesus said to them, '"Why are you troubled, and why do doubts rise in your minds? Look at my hands and my feet. It is I myself! Touch me and see; a ghost does not have flesh and bones, as you see I have." When he had said this he showed them his hands and his feet' (vv. 38-40).

The record says they 'still did not believe it because of **joy** and **amazement**' (v. 41).

 Extra comment

Back in the 1930s, a man claiming to be Jesus Christ visited Sydney. When this was reported in the local press, a group of Christians marched in procession to the hotel where he was staying, singing this hymn:

I shall know him, I shall know him
When redeemed by his side I shall stand.
I shall know him, I shall know him
By the print of the nails in his hand.

The elderly minister who recounted this event to me said that the imposter was 'quick to pack his bags and leave'.

JESUS APPEARS TO THOMAS

 Focus Passage: *John 20:24-29*

From time to time all of us experience doubt. This can be a 'good street to pass through but not one to live in'. On one hand, doubt can be destructive, on the other it is able to strengthen us when we are confronted with the evidence that dispels our doubt.

 Charting the action

Immediately preceding these verses, John records a visit by Jesus to the other disciples. Thomas, who was absent at the time, was sceptical of this, when the others reported their experience.

A week later Jesus appeared again and this time Thomas was present.

 ## Noting the emotion

Was **pessimism** a feature of Thomas' character? There is a glimpse of this when Jesus finally responded to the appeal from Mary and Martha to come to Lazarus' aid. Thomas gloomily said to the others of the apostolic band, 'Let us also go, that we may die with him' (John 11:16; see also John 14:5).

Faced with their report of the appearance of Jesus, Thomas is **adamant** that he will not accept their word that this has occurred. He bluntly spells out the evidence he would require before he could accept their testimony. Imagine their **exasperation** as they try unsuccessfully to convince him.

When finally Jesus appeared in that locked room (v. 26) Thomas' eyes must have almost popped out of his head as he stared open mouthed at the figure standing among them. This was no apparition; his eyes confirmed the evidence he demanded. Did Thomas tremblingly accept the invitation to touch those wounded hands or was the evidence of his eyes sufficient?

It is not recorded if he fell down before the Lord, but it is reasonable to assume that such action would fit with his **humble** affirmation of belief, 'My Lord [pause] and my God' (v. 28)

 ## Extra comment

It is helpful to recall that Thomas was present when Lazarus was called from out of his tomb. This, and the fact that Jesus had told them on more than one occasion that he would rise from the dead, should have made Thomas able to accept the testimony of his fellow disciples. However, I am glad that Thomas doubted, as what followed makes a powerful impact, helping to reinforce our Lord's word: 'The people who have faith in me without seeing me are the ones who are really blessed!' (v. 29 CEV)

JESUS AND THE MIRACULOUS CATCH OF FISH

Focus Passage: John 21:1-14

   Charting the action

'I'm going fishing.'
Seven shared in this fishing expedition but despite their skill their night's work was unproductive, 'they caught nothing' (v. 3).

Early in the morning they were hailed by a figure on the beach who advised them to throw the net 'on the right side of the boat and you will find some' (v. 6). When they did they were unable to haul in the net because of the weight of the large number of fish contained in it (v. 7).

Peter, recognising the stranger on the beach to be the Lord, dived over and swam to the shore. The others in the party followed, towing the net behind them. When they reached the shore, Peter returned to help them land the catch, which totalled in all 153 'large' fish (vv. 7-11).

'This was now the third time Jesus appeared to his disciples after he was raised from the dead' (v. 14).

   Noting the emotion

Perhaps it was due to **boredom** that Peter proposed the fishing trip. They may as well have stayed at home. The fish just weren't around. Why were they willing to accept the stranger's advice to try again on ' the right side'?

John had been present on the previous occasion three years before when something similar had occurred (Luke 5:1-10). Memory of that event must triggered his **excited** exclamation, 'It is the Lord!' (v. 7)

Were these words spoken in an awe-struck whisper or an excited shout?

Peter's reaction was instantaneous. 'Splash!'

His reported action of putting on his fishing coat to cover his nakedness is another of those touches that add reality to the record. He would not have swum in a heavy fishing coat unless it was for the sake of modesty. John also records a minor miracle, for despite the size of the catch, 'the net was not torn' (v. 11). This must have **surprised** him or he would not have bothered to record it.

Can you visualise the group as they gathered around that fire? Peter with his dripping wet coat and bedraggled hair and the others, huddling by the flames to warm up after the chilly night, Jesus offering them some of the fish that were already on the coals, 'and some bread' (v. 9).

John reports that none of them dared ask Jesus '"who are you? " They knew it was the Lord' (v.12).

Two of the group mentioned by name were Nathanael and Thomas. For Nathanael, here was one of the 'greater things' that the Lord told him he would witness when they first met (John 1:50). For Thomas, this miracle provided further evidence that Jesus was alive.

 ## For children

Try linking the two stories of a miraculous catch of fish. Recall of the first incident explains why recognition in the second was immediate.

JESUS REINSTATES PETER

 Focus Passage: *John 21:15-18*

 Charting the action

When his friends realised that it was Jesus on the beach, Peter dived overboard and swam to the shore. For a brief period they were alone. We have no way of knowing what transpired in their conversation, but now through John's record, we have insight into an important moment in Peter's life.

Commentators point out that in the original Greek of this passage, two different words are used for what the English versions translated as 'love'. '*Agapao*' is a strong word that could be translated as 'do you love me with all your heart', while '*phileo*' is a weaker word that could be rendered, 'I am fond of you'.

Kenneth Taylor has attempted to highlight this difference in the *Simplified Living Bible* text as follows:

'Simon, son of John, do you love me more than these others?'
'Yes' Peter replied, 'You know I am your friend.'
Jesus repeated the question.
'Simon, son of John, do you really love me?'
'Yes Lord' Peter said, 'You know I am your friend.'
Once more he asked him.
Simon, son of John, are you even my friend?'

With this third question the Lord used the weaker word for love instead of the stronger one. Taylor suggests that this was why Peter was troubled. 'Peter was upset at the way Jesus asked the question this third time.'

'Lord you know everything' he said, 'You know I am.'

 Noting the emotion

Because Peter's denial was threefold it seems probable that when facing Jesus' questioning he had this in mind.

When asked whether he loved Jesus with all his heart, the memory of his failure was too strong for him to answer by using such a strong affirmation of love. This is why he used a less forceful word.

When Jesus used the lesser word in framing the third question, 'Peter was **hurt**' (v. 17).

After each of his replies, Peter was given a commission, 'Feed my lambs.' 'Take care of my sheep.' 'Feed my sheep' (vv. 15,16,17).

This commissioning by Jesus had a **forceful impact** on Peter's subsequent ministry. Note the way he uses the shepherd and sheep analogy in his first letter found in the New Testament (1 Peter 5:2-4).

THE ASCENSION

Focus Passage: *Luke 24:50-53*
Other reference: *Acts 1:1-11*

The Apostles' Creed says:
'He ascended into heaven and is seated at the right hand of God the Father almighty from whence he shall come to judge the living and the dead.'

Notice the link the creed makes between the ascension of our Lord and the expectation of his return.

 ## Charting the action

The action is very briefly stated:
    'Jesus led them out to the vicinity of Bethany' (v. 50).
    'He left them and was taken up into heaven' (v. 51).
In Acts 1, Luke gives us slightly fuller detail:
The period between the resurrection and the ascension was forty days, during which time he gave them further teaching about the kingdom of God (vv. 1,3)

He commissioned them to be his witnesses (v. 8). Read Matthew 28:16-20 with this.

He was taken up and a cloud hid him from view (v. 9).

Two angels informed them that he will return 'in the same way you have seen him go into heaven' (Acts 1:11).

 ## Noting the emotion

The Acts account hints at the disciples' **surprise** at events as Jesus left them, for the men in white asked them why they were 'looking **intently** up into the sky as he was going' (v. 10).

Luke closes his gospel account with a description of them returning to Jerusalem 'with great **joy**' and them staying 'continually at the temple, **praising God**' (Luke 24:53).

We assume they were waiting **expectantly**, for the promised Holy Spirit, a promise fulfilled on the day of Pentecost.

Our Tools of Trade

Scriptwriters of 'TV soaps' know the importance of both action and emotion. Many focus strongly on action. Variations of the chase theme are endless. Sometimes it is the goodies chasing the badies, while on other occasions the baddies are chasing the goodies.

Some writers concentrate mainly on the interplay of emotion between the characters in their play. In studying the biblical incidents we too should watch for both action and emotion and try to portray these as we present our stories.

To do this we have four tools at our disposal. These are:
- Words
- Tone
- Expression
- Gesture

Words

Most of our message is communicated verbally, i.e. through words, and storytellers need to become connoisseurs of words.

Have you ever noticed how some words seem to have a fascination for particular people? My next door neighbour likes to describe things as 'unreal'. By this she means they are spectacular, but she chooses to use a more attention getting word. In similar vein, to say 'you're not wrong', carries a stronger intent than, 'you're right'.

In our storytelling learn to use **colourful words**. When Jesus indicated that he intended to dine with Zacchaeus, 'all the people began to mutter.' Isn't 'mutter' a delightful word. Not only does it conjure up for us the vision of a group of people chattering in low tone to one another but the word itself has a lovely sound.

'Gobble' is another word that attracts me. I pop it in whenever it is legitimate to do so. Perhaps the 5,000 that ate the loaves and fish snatched at the food offered and gobbled it down. After all, the Lord did say, 'these people must be hungry'.

Keep a pencil nearby as you read the biblical accounts and mark the colourful words. Let me demonstrate this with the story of the raising of Jairus' daughter in Luke 8.

Jairus came to Jesus **pleading** with him to come to his house. En route to Jairus' home the crowd was so intense that Jesus was **almost crushed** by it. The woman who touched his coat and caused the delay, came **trembling** and fell at his feet.

The crowd around Jairus' house was **wailing** and **mourning** for the girl.

When Jesus informed them that she was asleep, they **laughed** at him.

Each of these emphasised words is what I would term colourful and they give clear indication of the actions and emotions of the people involved.

Another important aspect to consider in the use of words is to recognise the force of **dialogue**. It fascinates hearers, so as the biblical record is littered with many gems of dialogue, as storyteller, slip dialogue in to the account wherever possible.

Take for example, the incident of the thieves crucified with Jesus. One is described as 'hurling insults' at him: 'Aren't you the Christ? Save yourself and us!' He must have been most surprised when his fellow thief told him off with the words, 'Don't you fear God, since you are under the same sentence? We are punished justly for we are getting what our deeds deserve, but this man had done nothing wrong. Jesus remember me when you come into your Kingdom.' Jesus responded to this request with, 'I tell you the truth, today you will be with me in paradise.'

In recounting this incident you cannot improve on the actual words used in the text.

A storytelling technique that seems to have been lost in recent times is to choose some **key words** around which to structure the lesson, thus providing a summary to aid students' memory. For example, you can plan the story of Bartimaeus around the key words of Darkness, Determined, Delivered. Using **alliteration** assists the memory.

In a series of Kids Club lessons entitled *Heroes of Faith* written for the Anglican Education Commission, I wove into each lesson the definition that faith was to **know** something, **believe** it, and **trust** yourself to it. Visiting a country school at a little town called Hawks Nest I told the children that the purpose of my lesson was to teach them what faith is. To my delight, one of the boys said, 'I know what faith is!'

'What is faith?' I asked.

'Faith is to know, believe and trust' he replied.

'Where did you learn that?'

'At our Kids Club!' was the reply.

Obviously the club had used the *Heroes of Faith* material. When I questioned him further I was encouraged to discover that he not only remembered the definition, but seemed to understand it.

Tone

Not only *what* you say but *how* you say it is important.

We all know how easily our attention wanes if the speaker's voice is flat, lacking in light and shade. As you prepare to recount the gospel stories, ask yourself, 'With what tone would this person or that have spoken?' then try to emulate that tone in your rendition of the event.

Sometimes the text will give you a pointer to the attitude of the person involved. As the thief on the cross is reported as 'hurling insults' at Jesus, we can assume that his question, 'aren't you the Christ?' was a sneer and render it in a similar way.

Mostly however, we must make our assessment of the tone by studying the context of the story and the way the speech is reported. Some time ago, a friend submitted for my assessment the draft of a play based upon the healing of the centurion's servant. I pointed out two simple errors that she had made, one relating to mood, the other to timing. The opening scene centred upon the doctor called to attend the sick servant. After announcing that there was nothing he could do and that he expected the patient to die, in the text of the play the character made a light hearted remark about sending his bill. This gave a wrong impression of the mood of the moment, which should have been very sober.

The second act centred on the centurion requesting some of the Jewish leaders to ask Jesus for his help. In this case the tempo needed to be one of urgency, but the text of the play was offhand and casual.

If you study the story with care, you will be able to assess correctly the tone you should use. It is through the tone of your voice that you describe both the mood and the tempo of the incident on which you are focusing.

You can use verbal **tricks or devices**. However, I hesitate to call them tricks, in case I give the wrong impression. The first of these is a **deliberate stammer**. For example, in the story where Jesus calmed the storm, as the occupants in the boat witnessed the storm die away, they are reported as saying, 'What kind of man is this? Even the winds and the waves obey him.' The storyteller can tell it like this:

'Wh-wh-what kind of man is this? E-e-even the winds and the w-waves obey him!' (Matthew 8:27)

In some instances the storyteller may choose to heighten the effect of something that is in narrative form in the record, by **switching** the incident **into dialogue**. For example, when Jesus appeared to his friends in the upper room, Luke reports that 'they were startled and frightened, thinking they saw a ghost' (Luke 24:37). You can switch this to, 'What's that? It's a g-g-g-ghost!'

Another device is to **emphasise personal pronouns**, placing strong stress on them. When Jesus asked the woman for a drink, she replied, '**You** are a Jew and **I** am a Samaritan woman. How can you ask me for a drink?' (John 4:9)

The **speed with which you speak** can also be important. When the parents of the blind man, as reported in John 9, arrived at the synagogue to identify him, they ran into a barrage of aggressive questions repeated in rapid style.

'Is this your son?'
'Is this the one you say was born blind?
How is it that now he can see?'

By contrast, the parents' reply was cautious, even hesitant and should be recounted much more slowly. 'We know he is our son, and we know he was born blind. But-ah-how he can see now or ah-who opened his eyes, we don't know. Ask him. He is of age, he will-ah-speak for himself.' Some 'ahs' sprinkled here and there give the impression of hesitancy.

Another storytelling device is that of **deliberate repetition**. When Bartimaeus called to Jesus for help, many of the bystanders rebuked him, telling him to be quiet, 'but he shouted all the more' (Mark 10:48). 'Jesus, Son of David, have mercy – have mercy – have mercy on meeeee!'

An exercise you could try is the story of the blind man referred to in John, chapter nine. Read it out loud attempting to emulate the tone you think the characters would have used. Some of the characters are reported as hesitant, others belligerent. Those addressing the parents are aggressive, while the parents reply cautiously and hesitantly. The healed man replies humbly but definitely. In the face of the belligerence of his questioners, he becomes cheeky, needling them with the question, 'Do you want to become his disciples too?' Their response is both vicious and indignant, but the man continues to irritate them and they become enraged. You may need to go down the back yard to try this out or your family may think you have gone crazy.

Another technique is the use of **the pause**. This is a means of heightening the suspense by pausing briefly at important moments. When the Lord shouted with a loud voice, 'Lazarus, come forth!' pause before describing what happened.

In reporting Thomas' reply to Jesus, heighten it in this way: 'My Lord (pause) and my God!' Or when Peter replies a third time, say, 'Lord you know everything (pause), you know I am your friend.'

Expression

'My face is my fortune, sir, she said'.

This is certainly true for the storyteller. You need to communicate astonishment, apprehension, exhilaration, despair and all of the other emotions to which we have already referred to with the expression on your face. We cannot afford to be expressionless and deadpan. Some people can practise expression in front of a mirror but I am too self-conscious to try this. I have, however, endeavoured to develop a 'rubber' face, mentally willing my face to depict the emotion I am describing.

Gesture

At a teacher training session I conducted, one of the delegates argued with me about the use of gesture.

'It's all right for you', he said, 'but I couldn't do all this gesture business!'

As he spoke, he used his hands vigorously.

'What do you mean?' I asked, 'you're doing it now!'

He looked embarrassed and put his hands behind his back. Going on, he had hardly said more than a few words before his hands were waving again.

'All I am suggesting', I said, 'is that you train yourself to use meaningful gesture.'

If you want to depict Bartimaeus begging from the passers by in Jericho, you could sit on the floor with your hands cupped, as though they were a beggar's bowl. Even an action as extreme as this is not overdoing it, providing it helps your audience feel the impact of the story.

An action is only faulty if it draws attention to itself, and your audience laughs at you rather than *with* you. If they laugh at you then you must tone it down. One of the factors influencing the use of gesture will be the size of your audience. In a small group, your gestures need to be more restrained than when you are addressing a large assembly. The important thing with gesture is to be natural, so don't overdo it. You are telling a story, not acting.

In saying this, there are occasions when you may choose to dress up and tell the story in the first person, from the viewpoint of either a major character such as Bartimaeus, or that of a minor character. The story of the storm on the lake could be told through the eyes of a passenger in one of the boats accompanying the disciples. As this person would not have been able to hear what was said, it would give an entirely different viewpoint to this account. The crucifixion through the eyes of Mary's sister would also give an interesting variation.

Our target

Sex is the topic of the first chapter of an excellent book by John Dickson, *A Sneaking Suspicion*. Had he put it further down in the list of topics, the author explains, many people would have turned to it first in any case.

By contrast, I have put these comments on target last, as many people would skip them if they were in the introduction. This does not mean that an understanding of our target audience is of lesser importance, for to my mind it should be our primary concern.

Mindful of the great commission, our endeavour must be to reach the greatest possible number of children and people with the message of the gospel. Statistically the church is failing to reach the younger generation. One only has to contemplate the decline in Sunday School attendance figures to recognise the truth of this.

In Sydney in the 1950s and '60s many Sunday Schools numbered hundreds of young people, now the average would be in the fifties or less. Some groups have preferred to channel their energies into after school Kid's Clubs instead of Sunday School and while this has brought some additional children into contact with Christian teaching, the larger mass of the population is unreached.

In New South Wales the opportunity to give regular religious instruction in the schools is still open, but this is not the case in every state. As a result, many children in Australian society are growing up with a very limited understanding of who Jesus is.

Australia, like many countries in the world today, is a multicultural society. People from other communities have introduced variety to our menus and also many varieties of faith. Wollongong boasts the largest Buddhist temple in the Southern Hemisphere. At Auburn, a Sydney suburb, you can visit a huge mosque complete with copper covered dome and minaret. A Baha'i temple dominates the escarpment in the Manly Warringah district, while at Woolgoolga on the north coast, a Hindu temple is listed as a tourist attraction. The prevailing viewpoint in the general populace is that this is good. After all, we are all going the same way aren't we? And does it really matter what label we wear?

In the face of this the Christian claim that our religion is uniquely different from all the others causes friction. Why do Christians make this claim? The answer is simple; we believe that the Lord Jesus was not merely another prophet with a message from God, but God himself. He claimed to be the Way, the Truth and the Life and asserted that no one could find salvation except through Him.

Parents in today's world are still eager that their children receive instruction in morality but prefer this instruction to be separated from what would be termed 'Christian dogma'. Our task is to show that those who give their allegiance to Jesus Christ find forgiveness and inner strength for daily living. It is for this reason that the account of His life, His death and resurrection must be the central theme of our teaching and preaching.

One of our early hymn writers expressed it this way:

> *God has given us a book full of stories*
> *That were made for His people of old.*
> *It begins with the tale of a garden*
> *And ends with the city of gold.*
>
> *There are stories for parents and children*
> *For the old who are ready to rest*
> *But for all who will heed them or listen*
> *The stories of Jesus are best.*
>
> *For it tells how He came from the Father*
> *His far-away children to call*
> *To bring the lost sheep to the Shepherd*
> *The most beautiful story of all.*

It is my earnest hope that this booklet will assist those who tell this 'beautiful' story to do so more effectively, so that many hearing it will be persuaded that Jesus is the Son of God and thus give Him their allegiance.

Commentaries Consulted

Bruce, F.F. *Matthew* (Bible Study Books, Scripture Union, 1971)

Cranfield, C.E.B. *Gospel of St Mark* (Cambridge Greek Testament Commentary Series, Cambridge University Press, 1963)

Morris, Leon *Luke* (Tyndale New Testament Commentaries, IVP/Eerdmans, 1989)

Tasker, R.V.G. *John* (Tyndale New Testament Commentaries, IVP/Eerdmans, 1989)

Nixon, Robin *John* (Bible Study Books, Scripture Union, 1968